GW00418108

Speak NOW

COMMUNICATE with CONFIDENCE

TEACHER'S BOOK

Jack C. Richards
David Bohlke
Carmella Lieske

OXFORD
UNIVERSITY PRESS

1 Speak NOW
Level Guide

Expand the *Speak Now* **Student Book lessons** with activities from the Multi-Skill Bonus Pack, available on iTools. This Level Guide provides you with a map of the course's various resources, allowing you to build a rich and comprehensive syllabus. Through targeted expansion activities, students gain confidence in English across every skill area.

Multi-Skill Bonus Pack Worksheets

VOCABULARY	READING AND WRITING	GRAMMAR Power Point™ Support	LEARNING OUTCOMES *Now I can...*
Greetings	University of America		
People	Homestay application	**A:** Contractions	...meet and greet people.
Communication	Communication 101	**B:** Tag questions	
Small talk	Hello from Brazil!	**C:** Polite requests	...ask about and give personal information.
Music	Friday Night Concerts	**A:** Present simple: *do* and *doesn't*	
Hobbies	Most popular travel movie 2003-2013		...express likes and dislikes.
Time	Train Service April-June	**B:** Compound nouns	...talk about and tell time.
Outdoor activities	Would you try jet skiing?	**C:** Prepositions in time expressions	
Family	Welcome to our home!		
Personality types	Portuguese tutor	**A:** This/That/These/Those	...ask about and describe people.
Fashion	Clothing Forever	**B:** Adjectives and adverbs	...give and respond to compliments.
Colors	The Perfect Look		
Daily routines	Mobile Phones before Bed		
Free-time activities	Students Don't Study as Much as "Should"	**A:** Information questions	...ask about and describe routines.
A typical day	What is your routine at work?	**B:** Present continuous	...ask follow-up questions.
School subjects	Greeting from New Zealand!		

Speak NOW
Level Guide

Multi-Skill Bonus Pack Worksheets

VOCABULARY	READING AND WRITING	GRAMMAR Power Point™ Support	LEARNING OUTCOMES *Now I can...*
My house	Vista Bay at the Commons	**A:** Prepositions of location	
In the home	Student's Suggestions	**B:** There is/ There are	...ask for and give directions.
My town	Lost cat	**C:** Where can I…	...ask for and give suggestions.
Around the city	To my place	**D:** What I like	
Prices and costs	Zurich is expensive!		
Items for sale	Bargaining tips	**A:** Adverbs of frequency	...ask about and bargain for prices.
At the newsstand	Media habits in Americans between 8 and 18	**B:** Modal auxiliaries	...ask about and describe frequency.
Descriptive adjectives	Your City Beat		
Food categories	Do you eat enough vegetables?		
Ingredients	Fresh from the Farmer	**A:** Count and noncount nouns	...ask about and describe quantities.
Food	Carrie's Café		...ask about and describe food.
Describing food	Pizza Pizza		
Last weekend	Thank you		
Time expressions	While you were out	**A:** Simple past tense	....talk about the past and future.
Reacting to news	Twice in the same day	**B:** Future time	...introduce and react to news.
Weekend activites	Summer classes		

Teacher's Book Contents

Teacher's Book Contents (continued)

The *Speak Now Testing Program CD-ROM* contains the following:

Spoken Interview Placement Test

Scoring Rubric and Testing Instructions

Quizzes

Quiz 1	Quiz 5	Quizzes Answer Key
Quiz 2	Quiz 6	Quizzes Audio Script
Quiz 3	Quiz 7	
Quiz 4	Quiz 8	

Speaking Assessment: General

Presentation Topics	Presentation Feedback Form
Interview Questions	Presentation Tips
Role-Plays	

Midterm Exam: Written; Speaking Assessment in the form of Standardized Tests

Midterm Written Exam	Midterm Exam IELTS™ style
Midterm Exam TOEFL® style	Midterm Written Exam Answer Key
Midterm Exam TOEIC® style	Midterm Exam Audio Scripts

Final Exam: Written; Speaking Assessment in the form of Standardized Tests

Final Written Exam	Final Exam IELTS™ style
Final Exam TOEFL® style	Final Exam Answer Key
Final Exam TOEIC® style	Final Exam Audio Scripts

Additional Teacher Resources

Speak Now 1 Video Scripts	Speak Now 1 Class Audio Script

TOEFL® and TOEIC® are registered trademarks of Educational Testing Services (ETS). This publication is not endorsed or approved by ETS.

How to teach a *Speak Now* lesson

Each lesson has five parts—Vocabulary, Conversation, Language Booster, Listening or Pronunciation, and Speak with Confidence.

Lesson Introduction

- Read the lesson title as students follow along. When applicable, have students answer the question.
- Point out the functions they will be studying. These are listed to the right of the lesson title.

1 Vocabulary

The purpose of this section is to get students thinking about the topic, activate their background knowledge, and introduce them to vocabulary that they will use during the lesson. To prepare the students to use the vocabulary, preteach it. When the vocabulary is unfamiliar to your students, present it through visual aids (for example, photos), actions, and gestures, and rephrasing or definitions.

- If necessary, have students use an English Learners' dictionary, perhaps before coming to class, to better understand not only the meanings but also how to use the words.
- Avoid giving students definitions in their first language. Although doing so may initially save time, students do not acquire the language as thoroughly and will rely on their first language rather than developing their English ability. In addition, nuances in languages often vary, creating additional complications as students continue to use the language.
- When you have time, further reinforce the vocabulary with personalization (for example, using the vocabulary in true sentences about themselves).

2 Conversation

There are two types of lesson patterns for the Conversation section. Some of the lessons follow the "Conversation with Substitutions" model and others follow the "Conversation with Changes" model. Teaching procedures for each lesson pattern are outlined below. Both conversations follow the same procedure for Part A.

Conversation with Substitutions

A

- This section helps students become comfortable with the topic and provides a model conversation that uses the functional language from the Language Booster section.
- Read the questions aloud. Ask the students to guess the answers by looking at the photos or illustrations. Ask students questions about details in the art.
- Play the audio and select students to answer the questions. If necessary, play the audio again.
- Make sure students understand the answers to the questions by asking concept questions or reforming the question to check understanding.

B

- Practice the conversation in Part A.
- Have students exchange the green and blue text as they practice the conversation again. This activity increases students' awareness of the different ways we can express the same idea.
- Encourage students to practice both roles and look at each other rather than their books.
- Students who finish the activities quickly can practice the conversation again using their own phrases and sentences.

In the second type of conversation, there are words and phrases highlighted in bold. Students are asked in Part C to listen for differences between the recorded conversation and the written conversation.

Conversation with Changes

A

Follow the same procedure as Conversation with Substitutions, Part A.

B

By practicing the conversation, students become more aware of functional language and more comfortable with language in "chunks". This prepares them for the Language Booster section and will also help them notice the changes in Part C.

C

- Tell students that they will listen to the conversation again, but the bold text has been changed. Explain that they should write the phrases and sentences that are different above the bold text.
- Play the audio. Check answers. If necessary, have students compare answers in pairs, play the audio again, and then check answers as a class.
- After checking answers, you may want to play the audio again so students can focus on the pronunciation and intonation. Also, have students pay attention to the words they did not understand before.
- Have students practice the conversation at least two times, once for each role.

3 Language Booster

A

This activity provides students with examples of the target language. In almost every lesson, the language includes both questions and responses. You may want to have students practice the language (i.e., take turns asking and answering the questions) before going on to Part B.

B

- This activity allows students to gain confidence as they use the language in short exchanges. This will provide them with the skills to make longer dialogues later in the lesson.
- In mixed ability classes, have students with lower English levels make some notes or sentence starters before they do the activity. These aids will help them to successfully complete the activity and further increase their confidence.
- After students have finished the activity, you may want to choose a few pairs to role-play the conversations in front of the class.
- After completing Part B, if students aren't confident with the language, have them continue practicing until they have more confidence. They can make even small substitutions to do this.

4 Listening

- The purpose of this activity is to help students focus on main ideas and details in the listening. Students may listen as many times as needed.
- After students have listened several times, you may want to stop the audio at key points so students can more easily complete the task.
- The Listening often concludes with a pair work activity that allows students to personalize what they have heard.

4 Pronunciation

- This section begins by helping students focus on pronunciation or intonation through listening. Students then practice the Pronunciation point. Students may tend to focus on the content and quickly forget to pay attention to their pronunciation and intonation. If this happens, briefly stop the class to remind students that they are practicing both content and pronunciation and then have them continue their practice.
- Play the audio, repeating as necessary.
- Ask students obvious questions to make sure they understand the point. For example, if you are teaching syllables, say some words and ask students how many syllables are in them.
- To give students more practice with the language, include all class (choral), group, individual, and substitution drills. This additional practice will give students more confidence and reinforce the pronunciation before they return to focusing more on content.

Speak with Confidence

- This activity allows students to use the target language as they accomplish defined tasks.
- Part A helps students prepare for their interactions in Part B.

Lesson Expansion

Vocabulary Worksheets

- After you have completed the Language Booster activities you can use the Vocabulary Worksheets for supplementary practice.
- The worksheets provide additional opportunities for students to practice the vocabulary and language studied in each lesson.
- Take advantage of the opportunities for additional speaking by having students compare their answers in class. Example conversations are often provided on the worksheets.

Reading and Writing Worksheets

- Reading and Writing Worksheets may be found on the iTools CD-ROM or on Oxford Learn, Oxford's Learning Management System. Access Oxford Learn with the code provided in the back of this book.

How to teach a review unit

Each review unit has two sections, *English in Action*, which includes a video, and *Speak Now*, which gives students the opportunity to role-play situations and review the language of the previous four lessons.

English in Action

- Video is a great way to introduce longer dialogues to students. The situational comedic videos showcase key vocabulary and functional language from the previous 4 lessons. Students can practice their comprehension skills and watch as the language functions link together in a complete dialogue.

- Using video is similar to teaching a listening or reading activity—there is a pre-video activity. On the *English in Action* page, this is called **Preview**. After this, there are "while you watch" activities. On the *English in Action* page, this is **Understand**. These activities include comprehension questions. These activities usually require two or more viewings. Finally, there is a post-video activity. On the *English in Action* page, this is **Discuss**.

- Before class, make certain your class Internet connection, computer, and projector are working.

1 Preview

- Students are asked to look at one or more photos from the video that they will watch in Part 2. With a partner, they talk about what they see. They also often make predictions.

- When possible, have students talk about what they see in more detail. For example, the Preview for Lessons 9-12 asks students to talk about people. Because students have recently studied describing people, you could have them brainstorm adjectives other than those listed.

2 Understand

During Part 2, students watch a video that recycles content, vocabulary, and language they have studied during the last four lessons. This allows students to see the material used in real-world situations and apply their learning more broadly.

A

- Explain what students must do (for example, they should number photos in Part 1 or listen and decide if their predications were correct).

- Play the video. Have students answer the questions in pairs or as a class.

B

- Part B asks students to listen for more details.
- Play the video and then have students answer the questions in pairs or as a class.
- Play the video again, as necessary, stopping to explain where an answer was within the dialogue.

3 Discuss

- The Discuss activity allows students to personalize what they saw.
- After students finish their discussions, have them do the **Confidence Booster** at the back of their books. This provides further reinforcement and review of the four units.

Speak Now

- In pairs, have students role-play each situation.
- After they have finished practicing, have some pairs role-play for the class.
- Remind students to assess their own abilities for each lesson. For any Lessons that they check *I need more practice*, encourage them to review the Language Boosters. (Pages are provided on the *Speak Now* review pages.)
- For a formal assessment, a testing CD-ROM accompanies this book.

Review Unit Expansion
Video Worksheets

- Video Worksheets with a cloze/gap fill activity may be found on the iTools CD-ROM or on Oxford Learn. Access Oxford Learn with the code provided in the back of this book.
- These worksheets provide additional listening practice for the English in Action video.

Grammar Support

- Grammar PowerPointTM presentations and Grammar Worksheets may be found on the iTools CD-ROM or Oxford Learn.

Speak Now Testing Program Overview

The *Speak Now* series helps learners Communicate with Confidence by using language accurately, fluently, and appropriately. The *Speak Now Testing Program,* found on the CD-ROM in the back of this book, allows teachers to perform a wide range of assessments—many in the style of popular standardized exams.

Speak Now's written and oral assessment tools can be customized to fit the needs of a range of program types and learning goals.

The Testing Program offers two main sets of tools:

1. **10 paper-based tests: 8 quizzes, 1 midterm exam, and 1 final exam** with listening that measure comprehension of the vocabulary and functional language of *Speak Now*;

2. a range of different types of questions, prompts, and topics for **speaking assessment**.

Teachers may choose to use any one or more of these materials alone or in different combinations. The **Scoring Guidelines** can be found on the *Speak Now Testing Program CD-ROM*.

Written Tests with Listening

There is a quiz for each 4-lesson unit of *Speak Now*. The **quizzes** are designed to be used after students have completed each group of four lessons and Speak Now review section in the Student Book. The quizzes have 10 items each. There is an audio track for the listening items in each quiz on the *Speak Now Testing Program CD-ROM*.

There is also a written **midterm exam** and a written **final exam**. These are designed to measure comprehension of the target language after students have completed Lesson 16 and Lesson 32 of the book, respectively. The midterm and final exams have 20 items each. There is an audio track for the listening items in each exam on the *Speak Now Testing Program CD-ROM*.

All answer keys and audio scripts are on the *Speak Now Testing Program CD-ROM*.

Speaking Assessment: General

The *Speak Now Testing Program* offers options for speaking assessment:

- **Interview questions** (a list of teacher-led interview questions)
- **Role-play cards** (cards for students to role-play situations in pairs)
- **Presentation topics** (lists of ideas for students to prepare and deliver short oral presentations related to the unit topics)

The *Speak Now Testing Program* features one set of the three speaking-assessment options profiled above for each unit or set of four lessons. Any or all of the speaking assessments can easily be used after students have completed a unit of work. To use these materials for midterm or end-of-term speaking assessment, simply choose from this list of materials, based on the units covered in the class.

Speaking Assessment: Standardized-testing Focus

The *Speak Now Testing Program CD-ROM* also offers speaking assessment in the style of popular standardized tests of English as a foreign language. For each **midterm exam** and **final exam**, you'll find:

- **TOEFL®-style speaking tasks**
- **TOEIC®-style speaking tasks**
- **IELTS™-style speaking tasks**

The goal of these standardized-testing tasks is to prepare students for the kinds of questions they would be asked on exams such as the TOEFL®, TOEIC®, or IELTS™ tests. As these materials are preparatory in nature; the rubrics do not reflect the type of scoring or grading that a test-taker would receive in a standardized testing situation.

TOEFL® and TOEIC® are registered trademarks of Educational Testing Services (ETS). This publication is not endorsed or approved by ETS.

Lesson 1 How are you?

Page 2
1 Vocabulary

A

Answers
Answers will vary. Sample answer.
First Name: Naomi
Middle Name: None
Last Name: Ootani

- Explain that *last name* can also be called *family name* since it is your family's name.

- If students don't have a middle name, ask them to omit it or make up a name they would like.

2 Conversation

[CD 1, Track 2]

A

Answers
Steve's last name is Hill.
Emma's middle name is Lori.

Point out that Steve and Emma shake hands in the third frame. Explain that how people introduce themselves varies between cultures, and that in many Western cultures, shaking hands is common when first meeting someone. Also explain that we sometimes shake hands when we see someone again after a period of time, but shaking hands is more formal and not often done between close friends.

Optional Question

Are Steve and Emma good friends? (No, they are meeting for the first time.)

B

Optional Activity

Have students practice the conversation again, substituting their own names.

Page 3
3 Language Booster

A

Tell students that *see you* is often blended together and said *seeya*.

Optional Activity

Ask students with whom they might use informal (for example, their friends) and formal (for example, teachers) language.

4 Listening

A

[CD 1, Track 3]

Answers	
1. informal	**3.** informal
2. formal	**4.** formal

Optional Activity

Have students identify elements of the informal language. (For example, in Number 1, the speakers say *Hey, Great* rather than a complete sentence, and *Yeah*. In Number 3, the speakers say *Hey* and *not bad* and ask *You?*)

B

[CD 1, Track 3]

Answers	
1. See you later.	**3.** Bye!
2. Good night.	**4.** Goodbye.

Optional Activity

Have students identify how one speaker says they need to leave. (Number 2: There's my bus. Number 3: I have to go. Number 4: Well, I'm off to work.)

5 Speak with Confidence

Encourage students to use formal language with you and informal language with other classmates.

After practicing, if you want students to use informal language with you in the class (for example, to call you by your first name), explain this to the students.

Lesson 2 Nice to meet you.

Page 4
1 Vocabulary

A

> **Answers**
>
> **Answers will vary.** Sample answer.
> - ✓ a classmate
> - ✗ a teacher
> - ✓ a friend
> - ✓ a neighbor
> - ✓ a relative
> - ✗ a colleague
> - ✗ a boss
> - ✗ a stranger

2 Conversation

[CD 1, Track 4]

A

> **Answers**
>
> Jesse lives in apartment 21.
> Tizzy is four months old.

Optional Question

Who or what is Tizzy? (Tizzy is Alex's cat.)

C

[CD 1, Track 5]

> **Answers**
>
> My name is => I'm
> I'd like you to meet => this is
> No problem. => No worries.

Page 5
3 Language Booster

B

Example conversation

A: Hi, everyone. My name is Chie.

B: Hi. My name is Sam.

C: Hello. My name is Massimo.

D: Hello. I'm Danielle.

A: This is Sam.

B: I'd like you to meet Massimo.

Optional Activity

Have students get into small groups. The first student introduces him-/herself and says one thing that he/she likes. If appropriate, increase the challenge by making students say something that starts with the letter of their name. The second student repeats what the first person said and then introduces him-/herself. Play continues until the first student introduces everyone in the group.

Example conversation

Anna: I'm Anna. / My name's Anna. I like apples.

Bob: This is Anna. She likes apples. I'm Bob. I like bikes.

Carl: That's Anna. She likes apples. This is Bob. He likes bikes. I'm Carl. I love cats.

4 Pronunciation

A

[CD 1, Track 6]

- Have students identify whether *to* combines with the word before or after it. (*To* combines with the word after it.)
- Have students indicate which sound is reduced (i.e., the *o* in *to* almost completely disappears).

5 Speak with Confidence

A

> **Answers**
>
> **Answers will vary.** Sample answer.
> My first name is Miguel.
> My last name is Lopez.
> I'm from Peru.
> I study at Tokyo University.

C

Optional Activity

After students have finished Part C, have them get into small groups and try to introduce all of the group members to the rest of the group. Encourage them to say one thing about each person (for example, where they are from or where they work/ study).

Example conversation

A: Hi, everyone. My name is Jae-sun, and this is Mark. He's a student at City College. That's Katie, and she's from Canada. And that's Raul. He moved here last month.

Lesson 3 Can you say that again?

Page 6

1 Vocabulary

A

Answers
Answers will vary. Sample answer.

__ write an e-mail   ✓ talk on the phone
__ write a letter   ✓ social network
✓ instant message   ✓ meet in person
✓ send a text   __ video chat

- If necessary, explain that a text is a message that is sent from a cell phone or smart phone device. Also explain that an instant message [IM] is a message that is in real time. IMs can be sent from computers and cell phones.

- You may want to explain that a social network is a group of people who write on the same Internet site. The people are often related in some way (for example, friends or people in the same kind of job).

Optional Activity

Ask students to say other ways they communicate with people (for example, a blog). If necessary, have students explain these forms of communication to their classmates. (For example, a blog is an Internet site where people write about their experiences and opinions.)

2 Conversation

[CD 1, Track 7]

A

Answers
Matt needs help with his homework. Joe's e-mail address is joe@newmail.com.

- You may want to discuss the importance of identifying yourself when making a phone call. For example, Matt could have said, "Hi, Joe. It's Matt." This would have helped Joe understand who was calling and avoid confusion.

- Explain to students that when saying e-mail addresses, we say words and abbreviations that can be understood. For example, we say *at* for the symbol @ and *dot* for any periods found in e-mail addresses. And we say *com* rather than spelling out c-o-m.

- You might want to have students practice saying e-mail addresses.

Page 7

3 Language Booster

A

Have students identify which expressions are more formal (Can I have your...? Can you give me your...?).

B

Optional Activity

Teach one response that students can use when they don't want to give the information (for example, Sorry. I'd rather not give that to you/say that.).

4 Listening

A

[CD 1, Track 8]

Answers	
a. 2 times	**b.** 1 time

B

[CD 1, Track 8]

Answers	
Delia	**Andy**
e-mail address:	e-mail address:
delia15@snmail.com	andy@245mail.com
cell phone number:	cell phone number:
968-8815	361-0018
work phone number:	work phone number:
752-9947	902-9914

5 Speak with Confidence

A

Explain that eye contact is important in English-speaking countries and encourage students to use eye contact as they talk to their classmates.

Lesson 4 Nice weather, isn't it?

Page 8

1 Vocabulary

A

Answers
Answers will vary. Sample answer.
✓ school ✓ movies ✓ family
✓ hobbies ✓ music ✓ money
✓ sports ✓ TV shows

2 Conversation

[CD 1, Track 9]

A

Answers
Chris and Maria talk about the weather, being busy, and music.
No, Maria doesn't like the song.

- Point out that Maria hesitates before saying *interesting*. Explain that this is one indication she doesn't really like the music.

- Explain that *interesting* can have both a positive and negative meaning. We often use interesting when we don't want to say something negative (for example, so we don't hurt the other person's feelings).

- Point out that after Chris says *I don't have much free time* (an utterance with *not*), Maria uses *neither* to agree. Maria does not use *either*. Help students remember this by pointing out that both start with the letter *n*.

C

[CD 1, Track 10]

Answers
It's really nice today => Nice weather
So, how are things at school? => How's life?
They're OK. => Things are OK.

You might want to point out that *How are things at school* is not as broad as *How's life*, which asks about not only school but also other things currently happening (for example, your family, your job).

Page 9

3 Language Booster

A

Point out the *isn't* in the tag part of the question. Have students notice that *is* is used in the response. If necessary, have students make other tag questions and responses (for example, This is a pretty nice place, isn't it? Yeah, it's fantastic.).

B

If necessary, have students make the questions before starting to practice.

Examples:

It's really sunny/cloudy, isn't it?

Beautiful/terrible, huh?

How's school/work? (Emphasize we usually don't say *your school/your work*. Have students provide the response: It's OK/great.)

Really hot/cold, isn't it?

You might want to teach a response to disagree (for example, Not really.).

4 Pronunciation

A

[CD 1, Track 11]

Emphasize that this intonation is used when the speaker expects the listener to have the same opinion.

5 Speak with Confidence

If necessary, have students brainstorm other expressions before they start.

Examples:

It's a little warm in here, isn't it?

You aren't in our class, are you?

You sit next to Collin, don't you?

Example conversation

A: It's a little warm in here, isn't it?

B: Yeah, it sure is.

A: Hi, you sit next to Collin, don't you?

C: Yeah. My name's Steve.

A: Nice to meet you. I'm Anna.

Lessons 1 to 4 Review

English in Action

Page 10

1 Preview

Answers
Answers will vary. Sample answer.
I think some people will talk in an apartment.
2 **a.**   4 **c.**
3 **b.**   1 **d.**

2 Understand

A

Answers
Answers will vary. Sample answer.
Yes, I did guess correctly. / No, I didn't. I thought d. was second.

B

Answers	
1. T	**4.** F (Maria and Jill are roommates.)
2. T	
3. F (Jill wants to borrow a broom from Eric.)	**5.** F (Tom is cooking.)
	6. F (Her number is 555-3992.)

You might want to have students correct the false statements. (See answers in parentheses above.)

Optional Questions

What does one second mean? (It means wait just a minute, please.)

What apartment do Jill and Maria live in? (They live in 3F.)

When are they going to eat dinner? (They are going to eat in about 30 minutes.)

What are Maria and Jill going to do until dinner? (They are going to clean their apartment.)

3 Discuss

You might want to have students give reasons for their answers to the questions in 2 and 3.

Example conversation

A: Do you know your neighbors?

B: Yeah.

A: Do you ever borrow things from people?

B: Not really.

Speak Now

Page 11

Provide an example of each conversation when necessary.

If many students need more practice with a particular lesson, you might want to review it in class.

1 *Example conversation*

A: Good morning, Max. How is everything?

B: Everything is great, thanks.

A: Have a nice day.

B: See you.

2 *Example conversation*

A: Good morning. My name is Leo Palace.

B: It's nice to meet you. I'm Collin Masters.

3 *Example conversation*

A: Excuse me. What's your name?

B: It's Peter Smithe.

A: And what's your e-mail address?

B: It's peter.smithe@newmail.com.

A: Can you repeat that?

B: Sure. It's peter.smithe@newmail.com.

A: Great. And what's your phone number?

B: It's 852-9136.

A: Can you say that again?

B: Sure. It's 852-9136.

4 *Example conversation*

A: Hi. Nice weather, isn't it?

B: Yeah, it sure is.

A: What are you up to these days?

B: I am really busy at school. How about you?

Lesson 5 I love hip-hop!

Optional Activity

Before students open their books, ask several of them if they like music (for example, Do you like music?). Ask them when and where they listen to music. (They might say, for example, in my room when I'm studying.) Then have students name some popular musicians and groups.

Page 12

1 Vocabulary

A

Answers
Answers will vary. Sample answer.

✓ rock ✓ pop ✓ country
✓ hip-hop ✗ classical ✓ jazz
✓ folk ✗ techno
✓ heavy metal ✓ reggae

You might want to have students name musicians they associate with each kind of music.

2 Conversation

[CD 1, Track 12]

A

Answers
Yes, he does. They both like hip-hop music. (Sandra also loves classical music.)

Page 13

3 Language Booster

A

Have students look at how to express dislikes.

- Explain that the position of *really* is very important, giving an example. *I don't really like jazz* expresses a mild dislike but *I really don't like jazz* expresses a strong dislike, closer to *don't like at all*.

- Explain that when Student A uses *not* to express a dislike (for example, I don't really like jazz.) and Student B agrees (i.e., has the same dislike), *Neither do I* is used. However, explain that when Student A says *I really dislike jazz*, students must agree by saying "So do I." Help students remember this by pointing out that *not* and

neither both start with *n* (i.e., both students use a word that starts with *n* or both don't use words starting with *n*).

4 Listening

A

[CD 1, Track 13]

Answers
3 **a.** rock 4 **b.** country 5 **c.** hip-hop 1 **d.** classical 2 **e.** jazz

B

[CD 1, Track 14]

Answers
a. S (both dislike) **b.** S (both like) **c.** D (male likes but female doesn't) **d.** D (female likes but male doesn't) **e.** S (both like)

To increase the challenge, you may want to have students also identify the opinion of each speaker. (See answers in parentheses above.)

5 Speak with Confidence

A

Answers
Answers will vary. Sample answer. 1. I like **hip-hop** a lot. 2. I don't like **classical** very much. 3. I really like **Lady Gaga** a lot. 4. I don't like **Shakira** at all. 5. I don't like *I Wanna Go*. 6. I don't really like **Mindless Behavior**.

B

If necessary, have students make the questions before getting into groups.

Optional Activity

Have students go around the classroom interviewing each other. When they've finished, as a class decide which kind of music is most and least popular.

Lesson 6 My favorite movie is…

Page 14

1 Vocabulary

A

Answers
Answers will vary. Sample answer.
__ sports   ✓ food   ✓ movies __ travel   __ video games   __ music __ books   ✓ shopping

B

You may want to encourage students to expand on their opinions by using the Lesson 5 Language Booster language and giving examples of the kinds of things in which they are and are not interested.

Example

A: Are you interested in sports?

B: Yes, I am. **I really like baseball and basketball.** Do you like video games?

A: No, I don't.

2 Conversation

[CD 1, Track 15]

A

Answers
Dan's favorite movie is *The Sound of Music*. Beth's favorite actress is Gong Li.

Optional Questions

What is the difference between an actor and an actress? (An actor is a man. An actress is a woman.)

Who is Dan's favorite actress? (He likes Reese Witherspoon.)

C

[CD 1, Track 16]

Answers
Who's yours? => What about you? My favorite is => I really like I'm crazy about => I particularly like

Page 15

3 Language Booster

A

If necessary, remind students to use who for questions about people and what for questions about things such as movies.

Point out that in response to the yes/no question (i.e., Do you like any bands in particular?), the response omits *Yes/Yes, I do*, but it can be understood.

B

Example

A: What's your favorite food?

B: I really like pizza. What about you?

A: I'm crazy about cheese.

4 Pronunciation

A

[CD 1, Track 17]

After students listen, point out that you and yours are said more strongly to help the listener understand that the speaker is asking for an opinion.

5 Speak with Confidence

Emphasize that students should continue to practice stressing *you/yours* as they talk with their classmates.

A

Before students start, you may want to ask students to identify what food is in the picture (sushi).

Point out that they may have several answers for each favorite.

Answers
Answers will vary. Sample answers. food: **pizza, sushi** TV show: **Big Bang Theory** sport: **volleyball, jogging** restaurant: **La Italia** celebrity: **J.K. Rowling** day of the week: **Saturday, Sunday, Friday**

Lesson 7 What time is it?

Page 16
1 Vocabulary

A

[CD 1, Track 18]

Students are probably unfamiliar with the second way of expressing time under clocks two, three, and four. After students have listened once, explain this way of telling time.

- Write 1/4 on the board and have students read it (either one-fourth or one quarter). Tell students that when we use *quarter* to tell time, we use *a* to mean *one*.

- Have students say how many minutes are in one-fourth of an hour (fifteen).

- Draw a basic clock on the board, with an arrow starting at the 12 and going to 6. Explain that we say how many minutes have passed since the hour started.

- Explain that we only use this way of telling time for 5, 10, 15, 20, and 25 after. Point out that saying *It's 18 after 8* is both difficult to say and difficult to understand.

- If necessary, remind students that we don't use *a* with numbers, so *It's a ten after twelve* is incorrect.

- Return to the clock you have drawn on the board. Draw an arrow from 12, this time going backward (i.e., past 11, 10, 9, 8, 7) to 6. Explain that when we pass thirty minutes after the hour, we say how many minutes are left until the next hour (because it is closer than counting from the hour that has passed). Have students read the second example under the last clock and notice whether the minutes or hour comes first (minutes). Tell students that we only use this way of telling time for times that are multiples of 5 (i.e., 35, 40, 45, 50, and 55). If necessary, practice these times.

- Have students deduce how to say 11:45. (It's a quarter to 12.)

- Tell students that it is important to understand this way of telling time to avoid misunderstandings. Write 1:40 on the board and have one student say the time. (It's twenty to two.) As the student says the time again, write 20 2 2 on the board. Say the time again writing 22 2. Point out that if they don't know *twenty to two*, they may not realize they are being told the time.

- After you've finished explaining, have students listen again before they practice.

2 Conversation

[CD 1, Track 19]

A

Answers
Ken and Zack are going to a concert. The train is at 6:15.

Page 17
3 Language Booster

Have students look at the *Telling exact time* column. Explain that *at* is used to give the time something will happen and is not used to give the current time.

4 Listening

A

[CD 1, Track 20]

Answers	
1. 11:00	**3.** 8:00
2. 2:50	**4.** 12:05

B

[CD 1, Track 20]

Answers	
1. no	**3.** no
2. yes	**4.** yes

5 Speak with Confidence

A

To make it more like a competition, give pairs the same amount of time. Then have the entire class close their books at the same time. When students have finished their conversations, have pairs say how many of the appointments they remembered.

Lesson 8 Would you try kayaking?

Page 18

1 Vocabulary

A

Answers
Answers will vary. Sample answer.

7	kayaking	8	snowboarding
2	skydiving	6	bungee jumping
5	skateboarding	3	rock climbing
1	jet skiing	4	surfing

B

Optional Activity

Before students begin, have them think of other words to describe activities (for example, difficult, easy, fascinating, scary, confusing, great).

2 Conversation

[CD 1, Track 21]

A

Answers
She thinks it looks really hard. She wants to walk around.

C

[CD 1, Track 22]

Answers
What do you think => How do you feel doesn't seem safe => seems dangerous bungee jumping => skateboarding

Page 19

3 Language Booster

A

Point out that we use and (fun and exciting) when giving two positive or two negative opinions. We use but (fun but dangerous) when one opinion is positive and the other is negative.

B

Have students refer back to page 15 if they are struggling with how to return the question.

Example conversation

A: What do you think of golf?

B: It seems kind of boring to me. What about you?

A: It looks fascinating to me.

4 Pronunciation

A

[CD 1, Track 23]

- If necessary, tell students that compound nouns are different than a noun with an adjective.

- Explain that a compound noun is a noun that combines two or more words. Emphasize that each word, by itself, has a meaning, but when the two words are combined together, the meaning of the compound noun is different than the meaning of each word separately. For example, the compound noun check-in is the process after you get to an airport or hotel, but check means the act of looking at something and in is used to show a location.

- Point out that compound nouns can be one word (for example, skateboarding) or two words (for example, jet skiing). Explain that some compound nouns are written with a hyphen (for example, check-in).

B

[CD 1, Track 24]

Answers		
1. **snow**boarding		2. **sky**diving
3. **river** rafting		4. **mountain** biking

5 Speak with Confidence

A

Answers
Answers will vary. Sample answer. individual activities: **running, weight lifting** group activities: **football, soccer** water activities: **swimming, water skiing** adventure activities: **scuba diving, paragliding**

Lessons 5 to 8 Review

English in Action

Page 20

1 Preview

A

Answers
Answers will vary. Sample answer. A good gift is a CD by her favorite music group.

2 Understand

A

Answers
They get Jill tickets to a new musical called *Dance City*. Yes, I did guess correctly. / No, I didn't.

B

Answers	
1. c	**4.** c
2. a	**5.** c
3. b	

Optional Questions

Does Tom like sports? (Yes, he loves them.)

Who likes heavy metal music? (Jill.)

What is Coldplay? (It's a band that Maria and Tom like.)

What time does the musical start? (It starts at 7:30.)

How did they buy the tickets? (They bought them on the Internet.)

3 Discuss

You might want to have students give reasons for their answers to Number 1.

Speak Now

Page 21

Provide an example of each conversation when necessary.

If many students need more practice with a particular lesson, you might want to review it in class.

In a mixed-ability class, have lower level students make the required conversations but encourage higher level students to provide reasons for their answers and expand the conversation (i.e., don't just follow a Question-Answer, Question-Answer, trade partners, Question-Answer, Question-Answer pattern).

5 *Example conversation*

A: I love techno. How about you?

B: I don't.

A: What kind of music do you like?

B: I really like jazz.

A: So do I. How about slow songs? Do you like slow songs? I don't.

B: Neither do I.

6 *Example conversation*

A: What's your favorite TV show?

B: I'm crazy about *Big Bang Theory*. How about you?

A: I love that show, too. So, do you like any ice cream flavors in particular?

B: I really like Swiss almond.

7 *Example conversation*

A: What time do you wake up?

B: At half past six.

A: What time do you go to sleep?

B: About eleven.

8 *Example conversation*

A: How do you feel about surfing?

B: It sounds dangerous to me.

A: What do you think of table tennis?

B: I think it's kind of boring.

Lesson 9 Do you have any brothers?

Page 22

1 Vocabulary

A

Answers			
1. f	**2.** c	**3.** e	**4.** b
5. d	**6.** a	**7.** g	

You may want to ask students what they call each parent (mom/mother, dad/father) and grandparent (grandma/grandmother, grandpa/grandfather).

B

Tell students that when they count brothers and sisters, they should not include themselves.

However, students should include themselves in counting the number of family members. (For example, How many people are in your family? Five. My mother, my father, my brother, my sister, and me.)

Optional Activity

A family tree is a visual representation of an extended family. The youngest generation is at the bottom of the "tree," and the oldest generation is at the top. A basic tree might look like the one below, with Nancy and Bob having one child, their son Steve. Steve is married to Sherry (shown by =), and they have two children, Lee and Nate. Sketch a simple family tree on the board and then use it to ask students questions. (For example, Who are Lee's grandparents?) With a more detailed tree, cousins and other vocabulary can be practiced.

Nancy = Bob

/

Steve = Sherry

/ /

Lee Nate

Have students quickly sketch family trees and then take turns asking and answering questions to practice the vocabulary.

2 Conversation

[CD 1, Track 25]

A

Answers
Teresa has three sisters. Her brother is 12 years old.

C

[CD 1, Track 26]

Answers
have no idea => don't know Why don't you get them => How about his => your brother's

Optional Question

How many brothers and sisters does Teresa have? (Four.)

Page 23

3 Language Booster

A

Optional Activity

Bring in a photo of your family. Have students take turns asking you questions to practice the questions.

4 Pronunciation

A

[CD 1, Track 27]

If necessary, remind students that a word ending in *s* (such as parents) does not have *'s* (i.e., not parents's), but instead just an apostrophe mark after the word. Since the pronunciation is the same as if there is no apostrophe, the listener must understand the *s/s'* by context.

5 Speak with Confidence

Students can bring in a picture of their family or share a photo from their cell phones. This may make the conversation more interesting and personal.

Lesson 10 She's pretty smart.

Page 24
1 Vocabulary

A

Answers		
Answers will vary. Sample answers.		
	You	**Best friend**
patient	✓	✓
friendly		✓
serious	✓	
shy	✓	
quiet	✓	✓
smart	✓	✓
funny		✓
confident		✓

2 Conversation

[CD 1, Track 28]

Answers
Lily and her sister are both friendly.
Lily's sister is patient, but Lily isn't patient at all.

B

Optional Activity

If your students have pictures of their brothers and sisters, have them practice the conversation again, substituting their real names, ages, and personalities.

Page 25
3 Language Booster

A

You may want to have students brainstorm other ways to talk about personalities.

Examples: cheerful, helpful, outgoing, reliable

B

Monitor the discussions and if students are being unkind to others in the class, point out those students' good points.

4 Listening

A

Answers		
1. P	**2.** P	**3.** N
4. P	**5.** N	

Answers could vary, if students consider someone who is, for example, extremely (too) generous. If this happens, encourage students to think more generally.

B

[CD 1, Track 29]

Answers
1. serious, friendly, patient
2. shy, quiet (They aren't sure if she is friendly or not.)
3. forgetful, funny

Optional Questions

Does Katy like the new math teacher? (Yes, she does.)

What is Katy probably going to do? (She is probably going to talk to Vanessa.)

What is Katy's example of Joey being forgetful? (He called her by the wrong name two times.)

5 Speak with Confidence

A

Answers
Answers will vary. Sample answer.
a babysitter: friendly, patient
a parent: strict, calm
a best friend: funny, creative
a teacher: smart, friendly

B

Increase the challenge by having students explain why they feel those traits are necessary.

Optional Activity

Have pairs think of other people and the personalities they need. For example, a police officer needs to be patient and smart.

Lesson 11   I love your shirt!

Optional Activity

Before students open their books, you may want to have students name some popular clothing stores in the area.

Page 26

1 Vocabulary

A

Answers
Answers will vary. Sample answer. d, f, i, j, l

Point out that *jeans* and *shorts* don't have an *a* and seem to be plural since they end in an *s*. Explain that these pieces of clothing do not actually have plural forms (i.e., we don't say *jeanses*). You may want to teach how to count jeans and shorts (i.e., a pair of, 2 pairs of).

B

If necessary, remind students that *this/these* are used when the clothes are near the speaker and have students identify when to use each (*these* with jeans and shorts, *this* with the other items in part A). Also remind students of *that/those*, which are used when the objects are far away.

Optional Activity

Bring in pictures of people and have students practice the conversation until they are comfortable with the vocabulary. Or, have students describe other people in the class. To make it more like a game, have students keep points, awarded to the first person who guesses correctly.

2 Conversation

[CD 1, Track 30]

A

Answers
Cindy likes the color of Rachel's shirt (She says the color looks really good on Rachel.). Rachel got the shirt from her sister.

C

[CD 1, Track 31]

Answers
I love your shirt! => That's a nice shirt! It was a gift from my sister. => I got it on sale. That's so nice of you. => Thank you!

Page 27

3 Language Booster

A

Have students identify what *it* refers to in the response (the shirt). Then have them guess how to respond the compliment *I love your jeans*. (For example, I like them, too. I got them on sale.)

4 Pronunciation

A

[CD 1, Track 32]

- The meaning of a sentence can change drastically, depending on the words that are stressed. For example, in they're my mother's the speaker may be correcting the other person's wrong statement that they're your sister's. However, they're my mother's emphasizes which one belongs to the speaker's mother.

- Teach students that in English, the important words (the words that emphasize what the speaker wants to say) are usually stressed. These are often nouns, the important verbs, adjectives, and adverbs.

- Less important words (called function words) are usually not stressed and often spoken more quickly. Examples include *the*, a, auxiliary verbs such as *is*, prepositions such as *before* and *as*, and conjunctions such as *while*.

B

[CD 1, Track 33]

Answers	
A: pretty, ring	B: love, belt, new
B: thank, gift	A: no, old, brother's

Lesson 12 What's she wearing?

Optional Activity

To review clothing from Lesson 11, before students open their books, have students say what some of their classmates are wearing.

Page 28

1 Vocabulary

A

> **Answers**
>
> **Answers will vary.** Sample answer.
> Fred's shirt is orange.
> His socks are purple.
> His shoes are red.
> His jacket is blue.

Optional Activity

Have students use these colors to describe other things.

Examples: Apples are red.

This desk is brown.

My pen is black.

B

You might want to teach vocabulary to describe patterns in clothing.

Examples: striped, polka dot, plaid, checked, print, solid, flowered

2 Conversation

[CD 1, Track 34]

A

Before students listen, ask them where Casey and Brad are (in a store) and what they are doing (looking at clothes).

> **Answers**
>
> Casey doesn't like the yellow shirt because she thinks Brad doesn't look good in yellow.
> She likes the purple sweater for Brad.

B

Remind students to practice speaking, not reading, by looking up from their books each time it is their turn to speak.

Optional Activity

Have students talk about which colors look good/ don't look good on them. Then have them practice the conversation again, substituting these colors.

Page 29

3 Language Booster

A

Point out that we use *wearing* for contacts and explain that we also use it for glasses.

4 Listening

A

[CD 1, Track 35]

> **Answers**
>
> **1.** c   **2.** b   **3.** a   **4.** d

B

[CD 1, Track 35]

> **Answers**
>
> **1.** friendly
> **2.** serious
> **3.** confident / pretty
> **4.** quiet

Optional Questions

What word describes the first guy's personality? (Shy.)

Does the guy in the second conversation think Randy's clothes are unusual? (Yes, he does.)

In conversation three, who is pretty? (Susan.)

What does the guy think of Gary's shoes? (He thinks they are cool, but different. / He likes them even though they are different.)

5 Speak with Confidence

You might want to teach other vocabulary so students can describe the clothes in more detail.

Examples: It has buttons. It has a zipper. It's long-sleeved. It has short sleeves.

Lessons 9 to 12 Review

English in Action

Page 30

1 Preview

A

Answers
Answers will vary. Sample answer.
Jill's mother is wearing glasses and a hat. Her father is wearing a hat and a black shirt. Jill's grandmother is wearing a scarf and helmet. Her mom looks friendly. Her dad looks serious. Her grandmother looks creative.

2 Understand

A

Answers	
1. c	**3.** a
2. b	**4.** d

B

Answers	
1. jacket	**3.** easygoing
2. and shy	**4.** 75

Optional Questions

Who is shy? (Eric.)

Who is wearing new clothes for the party?
(Jill and Eric.)

What is Jill like? (She's easygoing and creative [like her mother]. If students answer her mother, point out that the question asks what she is like, not who she is like.)

Is David coming to the party?
(No, he's not.)

3 Discuss

If some students are doing most of the talking, stop the discussion. Remind students that they can include everyone in the group by asking the quieter students their opinions (for example, by asking *How about you?*).

Speak Now

Page 31

Make sure students mark how well they can do each task. If many students need more practice with a particular lesson, review it in class.

9 *Example conversation*

A: Do you have any siblings?

B: No. I'm an only child. How about you?

A: I have one brother. He's 18.

B: Is he a student?

A: Yes. He is in college. Do you have any cousins?

10 *Example conversation*

A: What are two of your friends' names?

B: Natsuki and Yoh. Natsuki is a student.

A: What is Natsuki like?

B: She is serious but funny.

A: What is Yoh like?

B: Yoh is a student, like Natsuki, but she also works at a bank. She is always calm.

11 *Example conversation*

A: That's a great shirt!

B: Thanks. I got it yesterday. I really like your jacket.

A: Thank you. It was a gift from my family.

12 *Example conversation*

A: What is Marco wearing?

B: He's wearing a T-shirt, jeans, and tennis shoes.

A: What color is his T-shirt?

B: It's red. It's cool!

A: And who's wearing purple shoes?

B: Leah is. She is the only student with purple shoes!

A: I know. What color is Sam's sweater?

B: It's green.

Lesson 13 When do you get up?

Page 32

1 Vocabulary

A

Answers
Answers will vary. Sample answer.

  __ get up early   ✓ check e-mail
  ✓ watch TV   ✓ talk on the phone
  __ study   __ have lunch
  ✓ take a shower   __ exercise

B

You might want to teach the phrase *almost every day* and have students also discuss the things they do almost every day.

2 Conversation

[CD 1, Track 36]

A

Answers
At 8:30 he has a karate lesson. He finishes school at 5:00.

C

[CD 1, Track 37]

Answers
What time do you wake up? => When do you get up? wake up => get up Do you have time then? => Are you free? at 10:00 I start school => school begins at 10:00

Page 33

3 Language Booster

A

Explain that *late* may have different meanings for different people. For example, if A says, I went to bed late last night, she may be talking about 11:00, but when B says the same thing, he may be talking about 2:30 in the morning.

B

Optional Activity

Have students brainstorm other routines (for example, cook dinner, wash your face) and practice with these activities.

4 Pronunciation

A

[CD 1, Track 38]

- Explain that reduction occurs when it sounds like we combine two words into one.

- Explain that when reducing *do you*, students must do two things. First, they should blend the two words together (i.e., say them without a pause between them) instead of enunciating each word. In addition, they must change the pronunciation of the *o* in *do*.

- Tell students that as they combine these words together, their rhythm will become more natural. In addition, their ability to understand reductions will improve.

- You might want to explain that we often combine the Wh- question word with *do you*, so that the three words sound like one word. For example, it may sound like a speaker says *whaddaya* rather than *what do you*. This combination is particularly difficult since the *t* sound becomes a *d*.

B

Remind students to use *at*.

Example conversation
A: What time do you eat dinner?
B: At 8:30.
A: When do you finish class?
B: At 5:45.

5 Speak with Confidence

Example conversation
A: Do you have lunch at home?
B: No, I don't.
A: Do you watch TV at night?
B: Yes, I do.
A: Great. Let me write your name here. (How do you spell it?)

Lesson 14 When do you get there?

Page 34
1 Vocabulary

A

Answers
Answers will vary. Sample answer.

S go shopping   S go out to eat
S workout   A go to the library
S go to the mall   A watch sports
A watch movies   A take a walk

2 Conversation

[CD 1, Track 39]

Optional Activity

Before students listen, ask them if any of them go to the gym. If some do, have them talk about (using gestures as necessary) what they do there (for example, lift weights) and how often they go (for example, two times a week). Alternatively, have students brainstorm different activities they can do at the gym (for example, aerobics, ride a bike, row).

A

Answers
Laura runs (on the treadmill) at the gym. Sophie does yoga (at the gym).

B

Tell students that one of the reasons they practice these substitutions is that there are many different ways to say the same thing. Remind them that even if they tend to use the same question when they speak, it is important to recognize questions and sentences with the same meaning when listening.

Page 35
3 Language Booster

A

Tell students that follow-up questions often use the five W (i.e., who, what, when, where, why) and one H (i.e., how) question words. Have them think about why this is better than questions starting with *do*, providing the answer if necessary. (A yes/no response doesn't contribute as much to continuing a conversation.)

Optional Activity

Have students think of additional follow-up questions. This will help demonstrate the diversity that is possible.

4 Listening

A

[CD 1, Track 40]

Answers	
3 **a.**	4 **d.**
1 **b.**	5 **e.**
6 **c.**	2 **f.**

B

Answers
Answers will vary. Sample answers.

1. What do you do in the library?
   Can you use the Internet in the library?
2. Where do you walk?
   Do you walk in the same area every night or do you go to different places?
3. How many hours a night do you usually watch TV?
   Do you usually watch TV alone or with someone? (Who do you watch TV with?)
4. Where is the new mall?
   How do you go to the mall?
5. Where is the café?
   What's the name of the café?
6. Who's your favorite player?
   What's your favorite team?

Optional Activity

After pairs think of questions, have them share their questions with the class. As a class, decide which questions will elicit longer conversations.

5 Speak with Confidence

A

Emphasize that students should only write notes. This will help them practice speaking, rather than reading, in Part B. However, if you have a mixed ability class, you may want to allow lower level learners to write more complete thoughts.

Lesson 15   What do you do first?

Page 36
1 Vocabulary

A

Tell students that they can use the days of the week and time phrases many times.

> **Answers**
>
> **Answers will vary.** Sample answer.
> I get up early on Sunday mornings.
> I stay up late on Friday nights.
> I go out with friends on Sunday afternoons.
> I don't do much on Saturday nights.
> I feel my best on Thursday mornings.
> I feel my worst on Tuesday mornings.

Optional Activity

Take a class poll to find out when most students do each activity.

2 Conversation

[CD 1, Track 41]

A

> **Answers**
>
> Derek meets some friends on Sundays.
> He goes to an outdoor market in the park.

C

[CD 1, Track 42]

> **Answers**
>
> on Sundays => first
> Then what do you do? => What do you do next?
> Yeah, I like that place. => What do you do after that?

Point out that the third substitution is a change from a statement to a question, but the response remains the same.

Page 37
3 Language Booster

A

Point out that all the verbs are simple present. Explain that this is because we're talking about routines, not something that's happening right now.

B

- Emphasize that they will need the notes later so they must take them.
- Explain that *later* suggests some time passes between the activities, and it is possible that some unmentioned activities occur in between the activities that are mentioned.
- Emphasize that students don't have to say the activities in the order of the chart.

Example conversation

A: Well, in the mornings, first I get up. Then I take a shower. After that I check e-mail. I don't eat breakfast until later, maybe 10:00. After school, first I do my homework. Then I have dinner. Later I watch about 30 minutes of TV before I go to bed.

4 Pronunciation

A

[CD 1, Track 43]

Have students notice the secondary stress within the sentence, and then explain that the next most important information is often stressed. If necessary, have students identify this (i.e., breakfast, run, shower).

B

Students should use their notes about their partner's routine (written in Part 3 B).

5 Speak with Confidence

B

Have students focus on their pronunciation as they do the activity.

Example conversation

A: So what do you do Friday nights?

B: Well, first I go home and eat dinner. Then I go to my friend's house. We talk and eat snacks like ice cream. Later, we listen to music.

A: Sounds fun. How about you, C? What do you do first on Friday nights?

C: Well, first I meet friends outside of the library and we go out for dinner. Then we go to the mall to shop. After that, we go to a coffee shop.

Lesson 16 What are you doing?

Optional Activity

Before students open their books, ask students what their majors are, or what they majored in/would like to major in.

Page 38

1 Vocabulary

A

Read the class names so students become familiar with their pronunciation. You may want to point out that the *p* is silent in psychology.

Answers			
Answers will vary. Sample answer.			
B	statistics	BE	history
B	economics	E	sociology
BE	math	B	marketing
E	psychology	B	management
BE	English	E	literature

B

Emphasize that opinions cannot be wrong even when they are different. Tell students that B uses *actually* to point out their difference in opinion. Explain that *actually* should not be used if they have the same opinion.

Optional Activity

Have students talk about which classes they have to (had to/will have to) take for their major.

2 Conversation

A

[CD 1, Track 44]

Answers
Greg wants to go to a movie. / He wants to watch a movie.
Emi is learning modern dance/tap dance.

Page 39

3 Language Booster

A

Point out that the grammar is the same as that used to discuss activities that are currently being done (for example, I'm studying math right now.).

4 Listening

A

[CD 1, Track 45]

Answers		
	Manuel	Claire
rehearsing for a play		✓
studying for midterm exams	✓	✓
saving money for a trip	✓	
teaching French		✓

B

[CD 1, Track 45]

Answers
1. The play starts next week.
2. He works two nights a week.
3. Claire is teaching her neighbor (a person who lives near her).

Optional Activity

Remind students that it is important to guess the meaning of a new word by using the context. Have students listen for the word *performance* and reword it (for example, show).

Have students listen for the word *rehearsing* and reword it (for example, practicing).

Optional Questions

Who is really busy? (Both Claire and Manuel are.)

Is the play that Claire's in funny? (Yes. She says this, and it is a comedy.)

Is Manuel going to go to Claire's play? (Yes, he is.)

Does Manuel want to study French with Claire? (Yes, he does.)

5 Speak with Confidence

B *Example conversation*

A: This person is watching a lot of TV.

B: Is it Jae-soon?

C: No, it's not me. Is it you, David?

D: Yes, it's me.

A: What shows are you watching?

Lessons 13 to 16 Review

English in Action

Page 40

1 Preview

A

Answers
Answers will vary. Sample answer.

a. doing homework   **c.** swimming
b. playing volleyball   **d.** going out to eat
I do homework and go out to eat most weekends.
I rarely play volleyball or go swimming.

2 Understand

Answers

1. Saturdays   **3.** delicious
2. 7:30   **4.** 45

3 Discuss

Answers
Answers will vary. Sample answer.

1. Eric is busy and doesn't want to exercise with Jill. Jill likes to exercise.
2. No, I don't./Yes, I do. I love to swim.
3. My favorite day of the week is Saturday. I usually get up late. Then I watch TV. Later, I have a big lunch. Then, I go shopping with friends. In the evening, I go to a movie.

Optional Activity

Have students talk about what Eric probably does on Sunday morning (for example, sleep). Also have them discuss whether they would like to spend Sunday morning with Jill, giving reasons for their answers.

Speak Now

Page 41

13 *Example conversation*

A: What time do you get up?
B: I usually get up at 7:00.
A: OK. And what do you do after you get up?
B: I make coffee.
A: Do you study in the morning?
B: No, I don't. I usually study after dinner.
A: I see. Do you have lunch at school?
B: No, I don't. I usually eat before I go to school.

14 *Example conversation*

A: I work every day.
B: Really? Where do you work?
A: I work in the cafeteria. I also take a walk every day.
B: Every day? Why?
A: It helps me relax. And I study every morning.
B: Do you study on the weekends, too?
A: Yes, I do.

15 *Example conversation*

A: On a busy day I usually get up at 7:00.
B: What do you do after that?
A: I get ready and leave. I leave my house by 8:10.
B: Then what do you do?

16 *Example conversation*

A: What are you doing these days?
B: I'm learning how to play the piano. I'm also taking golf lessons.
A: Cool. Are you taking any interesting classes this semester?
B: I'm taking Chinese. It's really hard, but it's very interesting.

Lesson 17 What's your place like?

Page 42

1 Vocabulary

A

Explain that your place means the place where you live.

Answers
Top of apartment, left to right: 6, 3, 1, 5 Outside the apartment: 7 Bottom of the apartment, left to right: 2, 4

Optional Activity

Have students talk about whether the apartment is typical for their area. (For example, In our country, there usually isn't a laundry room in an apartment.)

2 Conversation

[CD 2, Track 2]

A

Answers
Andy thinks the location is good./ Andy likes his apartment because it is convenient. There are four rooms.

Optional Activity

Have students talk about whether they would rather have a small but conveniently located apartment or a large but less conveniently located apartment, giving reasons for their answers.

B

Optional Activity

Have students practice again substituting real information about their apartments.

Page 43

3 Language Booster

You might want to have students think of other substitutions for the first question (for example, bedroom, kitchen).

B *Example conversation*

A: What's your apartment like?

B: It's small and not very convenient.

A: Is there a laundry room?

B: No, there isn't. How about your place? What's it like?

4 Listening

A

[CD 2, Track 3]

Answers	
1. ✓	3. (The living room is the bedroom.)
2. ✓	4. (It does not have a laundry room.)

B

[CD 2, Track 3]

Answers
Students should write two of the following: it's nice, it's comfortable, the yard, it's quiet

C

Encourage students to give reasons for the things they like about their homes.

Example conversation

A: I really like my living room. It's big. And my place is very convenient. I can walk to school in 3 minutes.

B: That's cool.

A: How about you? What's your place like?

B: I like my apartment because there's a laundry room in it. Many apartments don't have a laundry room. And I like my apartment because it's small. I can clean it in an hour!

5 Speak with Confidence

If necessary, have students brainstorm their questions and information in pairs but then do Part B with a different person to make the conversation more original.

Lesson 18 Where can I get a lamp?

Page 44
1 Vocabulary

A

Explain that a coffee table is a short table that is often in front of a sofa. To help students remember the name, you may want to act out someone sitting on a sofa, drinking a cup of coffee, and then setting it on the table.

Explain that a lamp can sit on the floor or on a surface such as a table. In more advanced classes, compare this to a light, which is built into the wall or ceiling of a room.

Answers
Answers will vary. Sample answer. living room: a sofa, a TV, a lamp, chairs, a coffee table kitchen: a refrigerator, a TV, a stove, chairs, a dishwasher bedroom: a bed, a dresser, a TV, a lamp, chairs, shelves, a closet

B *Example conversation*

A: In a living room, I think there is a sofa and chairs, a TV, a lamp, a coffee table, and shelves.

B: I don't think there are shelves.

2 Conversation

[CD 2, Track 4]

A

Answers
Raul needs a sofa, shelves, and a TV. *Manning's* sells shelves and things for the kitchen.

You may want to explain that something that is used is not new.

Optional Activity

Raul asks, "Where can you get shelves?" Explain that using you is a way of asking a general question. Raul is not asking Sam where he (personally) will buy them. Have students reword the question to make it more specific (Where can I get shelves?).

Page 45
3 Language Booster

B

You might want to have students give reasons for their answers, referring to Conversation, where Sam says, "Their prices are good."

4 Listening

A

[CD 2, Track 5]

Answers		
2	**a.**	a lamp
4	**b.**	a TV
3	**c.**	a dresser
1	**d.**	chairs

B

[CD 2, Track 5]

Answers		
c	**1.**	*The Furniture Depot*
b	**2.**	*Tech Town*
d	**3.**	*Walt's World*
a	**4.**	the outdoor market

C *Example conversation*

A: You can get a lamp at the mall and *Tech Today*.

B: You can also get one at *Lights Are Us*. But I think the best place to get a lamp is *Light World*.

5 Speak with Confidence

A *Example conversation*

A: Where's a good place to buy unusual clothes?

B: How about *Turnaround*?

C: I would go to *Pink*.

D: The best place to get unusual clothes is *Dana's*.

A: Oh, yeah. I think so, too. So, how about comic books? Where can I find new comic books?

Lesson 19 Where's the mall?

Page 46

1 Vocabulary

A

Answers
Answers will vary. Sample answer.

✓ bank	✗ drugstore	✗ hair salon
✓ movie theater	✓ mall	✓ library
	✗ post office	✗ department store

B

Optional Activity

Have students talk about other activities they do in each of the places in Part A. For example, I usually eat dinner at the mall. There are lots of different places.

2 Conversation

[CD 2, Track 6]

A

Answers
The post office is on King Street. There's a hair salon called *Freddy's* on University Avenue.

Optional Activity

Tell students that every street in the United States has a name, no matter how short the street is. You might want to explain that in addition to streets and avenues, there are drives, circles, courts, and boulevards. (Boulevards are usually wide and often have something down the center between the lanes, which go in two directions.)

C

[CD 2, Track 7]

Answers
send these postcards => mail these letters across from the park => next to the library on University Avenue => in the mall

Page 47

3 Language Booster

A

Optional Activity

Have students practice the language, substituting real locations, for example, near the school.

Example conversation

A: Where's the nearest supermarket?

B: It's across from the school.

B

As students follow along, read the street names. Point out that the streets go up and down and the avenues go right to left. Also point out that the avenues are in numerical order (i.e., First, Second, Third).

Optional Activity

Teach additional language to allow students to be more specific.

It's on the corner (of Third Avenue and Elm Street).

It's in the middle of the block.

It's just down the street.

4 Pronunciation

A

[CD 2, Track 8]

B

Explain that students should not pay attention to spelling, but instead must focus on the sounds. For example, the final e in *where* is silent, creating linked sounds between the r (consonant) and the e (vowel) in *exactly*.

5 Speak with Confidence

B *Example conversation*

A: Where's the nearest ATM?

B: There's one in the drugstore.

A: Where's the drugstore?

B: It's on Elm Street, next to the movie theater.

Lesson 20 Take a left.

Page 48

1 Vocabulary

A

Answers
Answers will vary. Sample answer.
__ a stadium   ✓ a bridge   __ a park __ a river   ✓ a subway   __ a freeway ✓ a bus stop   station   __ a taxi stand

Optional Activity

Have students say different activities they do at the places. For example, I can watch a baseball game in a stadium.

B

Optional Activity

Explain that some freeways are called highways or expressways. Also explain that turnpikes are like highways but usually charge a toll (i.e., money to drive on them).

2 Conversation

[CD 2, Track 9]

A

Answers
Anna is having a birthday party (for herself) on Sunday. Her address is 122 Pine Street.

C

[CD 2, Track 10]

Answers
I'd love to. => That sounds great! not far=> really close Can you give me directions? => How do I get there? Take a => Turn

Optional Questions

What is Anna's apartment number? (14C)

What time does the party start? (It starts around 6:00.)

Page 49

3 Language Booster

A

If necessary, explain that *asking for clarification* means to get more (specific) information or to make sure of something.

Optional Activity

Using desks as blocks/corners, have students take turns giving directions while you (or a student) follow the directions (i.e., walk around the classroom) and ask for clarification.

B

After giving directions once, you may want to encourage students to start at the new location (i.e., the place they just got directions to), rather than always returning to the X. This will allow them to practice more varied conversations.

4 Pronunciation

A

[CD 2, Track 11]

- Explain that the intonation and stress help the speaker point out that he/she has two different ideas and would like to know which one is correct.
- Explain that students should use pauses carefully, with a pause before *or*.
- Tell students they should also chunk the information. In other words, they should try to say each idea as a smooth phrase (for example, turn right, turn left). They should try not to have long pauses within each phrase (for example, not say *turn* [pause] *right*).
- Point out that the speaker also says the choices with a little more emphasis (i.e., more strongly) to help the listener understand the choices.

5 Speak with Confidence

If students are having difficulty giving directions without looking at something, have them sketch a rough map and then start again.

Lessons 17 to 20 Review

English in Action

Page 50

1 Preview

Answers
Answers will vary. Sample answer. **1.** I think they need almost everything since they only have a desk and chair. / They need a table, chairs, and a TV. **2.** I don't think Maria and Tom like the same furniture.

2 Understand

A

Answers
Maria needs to buy 1. a bed, 2. some chairs, and 3. a bookcase.

B

Answers
1. *Larson's* is the tall brown building at the top of the map on First Avenue. **2.** *The Superstore* is the white building with yellow, in the middle of the map. **3.** *Pace Supermarket* is across from *The Superstore*. *Pace Supermarket* is a reddish-orange color. **4.** *Market Fair* is by the park, on the bottom left side of the map.

3 Discuss

Answers
Answers will vary. Sample answer. **1.** No, friends shouldn't buy each other household items because your friend may not like what you pick out. **2.** Every apartment needs a bed, a table, a couch, and a TV. **3.** Students should practice asking for and giving directions. (See *Example conversation* below.)

Example conversation

A: I'm at *Larson's*. How do I get to the *Superstore*?

B: Go down First Avenue. Turn right at the corner of West Avenue and First Avenue. Go straight. It's on the corner of West Avenue and Mason Street.

Speak Now

Page 51

Provide an example of each conversation when necessary.

17 Example conversation

A: What's your home like?

B: It's too small. I want a bigger place.

A: How many rooms are there?

B: Just two, the living room and the bathroom. But it's easy to clean, and it's very close to school.

18 Example conversation

A: I want a new cell phone. Where's a good place to get one?

B: The best place to get one is *Phones for You*.

A: Great. And where can I find a dresser?

B: How about looking in the school newspaper? Sometimes students sell things they don't need.

19 Example conversation

A: Where's the nearest ATM?

B: It's next to the cafeteria.

A: Thanks. And is there a drugstore around here?

B: Yeah. It's next to the school, on School Street.

20 Example conversation

A: How do I get to the stadium?

B: Go straight down School Street. It's on the corner of School and First.

A: Is that First Street or First Avenue?

B: First Street.

A: Thanks. And how do I get to the city library? I have to write a report.

B: Go down School Street. Turn left at the corner in front of the train station.

A: What's it near?

B: It's by the Greek restaurant.

Lesson 21 How much is coffee?

Page 52
1 Vocabulary

A

Answers
Answers will vary. Sample answer.

$20	a haircut
$3.75	a cup of coffee
$50	a taxi ride across town
$10	museum admission fee
$13	a movie ticket
$2	bus fare

2 Conversation

[CD 2, Track 12]

A

Answers
Coffee is one dollar in a convenience store.
Coffee in a coffee shop is not cheap.

- Explain that there are one hundred cents in one dollar. This is important in countries that don't have smaller and larger units of their currency.

- Tell students that when saying prices with dollars and cents, they should either say both *dollars* and *cents* (for example, two dollars and fifty cents) or neither *dollars* nor *cents* (for example, two fifty). Emphasize that they should not say only one of the two words. For example, it is incorrect to say *two dollars fifty*, and *two and fifty cents* is also wrong.

- Tell students that *a dollar* is the exception because *a* rather than a number is used. Point out that *a dollar fifty* is used in the conversation.

C
[CD 2, Track 13]

Answers
That's reasonable. => That seems fair.
can be=> costs around
They cost => They're

Ask students to explain the difference between *can be six dollars* and *costs around six dollars*, providing the answer if necessary. (*Can be six dollars* suggests that the most coffee costs is six dollars and that some coffee is not this expensive. *Costs around six dollars* implies that most coffee in nice coffee shops is usually six dollars.)

Optional Question

Is Eduardo probably from the same town as Greg? (No. He doesn't know the prices, and he says *your town.*)

Page 53
3 Language Booster

B

Example conversation

A: How much does a meal at a fast-food restaurant cost?

B: It's around six dollars.

4 Pronunciation

A
[CD 2, Track 14]

Explain that we generally stress the first sound (i.e., syllable) of multiples of ten (i.e., thirty, forty, fifty, etc.).

Tell students that even native speakers sometimes misunderstand numbers that sound similar (for example, 13 and 30), but that by practicing the correct stress, they will be better able to both say and understand the numbers.

B
[CD 2, Track 15]

Answers	
1. $1.70	**3.** $16.17
2. $40.50	**4.** $19.90

5 Speak with Confidence

A

If students don't know the prices, have them guess.

Lesson 22 Will you take $20?

Page 54

1 Vocabulary

A

Answers
Answers will vary. Sample answer. __ clothes __ makeup ✓ furniture __ electronics ✓ CDs __ video games ✓ toys __ sports equipment

2 Conversation

[CD 2, Track 16]

A

Answers
Luke offers Zoe $20 for the lamp. They agree on $25.

Explain that *give it to you* does not mean *give for free* but instead emphasizes the speaker's belief that the price is low.

Optional Activity

Explain that Luke and Zoe negotiated the price rather than Luke paying the price Zoe originally said. Have students talk about whether bargaining is common in their area. If it is, have them talk about who bargains (for example, usually people in markets), when (for example, on market days), and what for (for example, anything in a market).

If bargaining isn't popular in the area, have students talk about the advantages (for example, it can be fun, you can buy things for a lower price) and disadvantages (for example, it can be frustrating, you might pay more than other people) of bargaining.

Page 55

3 Language Booster

A

If necessary, have students make the third question for situations when there are two or more things. (Will you give them to me for $20?)

4 Listening

A

[CD 2, Track 17]

Answers
4 **a.** CDs 1 **b.** a computer bag 3 **c.** a bowl 2 **d.** sunglasses

B

[CD 2, Track 17]

Answers	
1. $50	**3.** $115
2. $12	**4.** $20 for all of the CDs

C

If there aren't any regular markets in the city, have students think about markets during festivals or make up their answers.

Example conversation

A: We don't have outdoor markets.

B: I know. I wish we did. But there are markets during the summer festivals.

A: That's true. I always buy a snow cone.

B: It's a good place to buy used clothes, too.

A: But there's no bargaining.

B: Yeah, but that makes it easier to choose which clothes I want.

5 Speak with Confidence

B *Example conversation*

A: How much is this black jacket?

B: It's $75.

A: That's expensive. A new one is $85. Will you take $35?

B: No, but I can give it to you for $70.

A: No, thanks. I'll keep looking.

Lesson 23 Do you ever buy books?

Page 56

1 Vocabulary

A

Answers
Answers will vary. Sample answer.

N newspapers   N magazines
S candy   N gum
N energy drinks   S vitamins
N flowers   N phone cards

Optional Activity

Have students get into small groups and write as many things as they can that they buy often. When time is up, have groups count the number of things they wrote, and determine the winning group. Have groups share their ideas with the class.

2 Conversation

[CD 2, Track 18]

A

Answers
Lian buys fashion and interior design magazines. Lian keeps all of the magazines.

If necessary, explain that interior design has to do with how to decorate and use the area in rooms and buildings.

C

[CD 2, Track 19]

Answers
I buy lots of magazines. => I often buy them. What kind => Which ones Every week. => Twice a week.

Ask students to discuss the difference between *what kind* and *which ones*, providing the answer if necessary. (For example, the response to the kind of magazine can be broad—the topic of the magazines, while the response to *which ones* can be quite specific—the names of magazines.)

Optional Question

Why does Lian's mom probably think Lian is crazy? (Perhaps because magazines are so expensive, yet Lian buys them very often.)

Page 57

3 Language Booster

A

If students are familiar with the grammar *have you ever...*, ask them to explain the difference, providing the answer if necessary. (For example, *have you ever* asks about a past experience, while *do you ever* asks about actions that repeat.)

4 Pronunciation

A

[CD 2, Track 20]

B *Example conversation*

A: Do you ever buy comics?
B: No. I think they are too expensive. How about you? Do you ever buy celebrity magazines?

Optional Activity

Give students more questions to discuss, having them focus on intonation as they ask the questions.

How often do you go shopping?
Do you ever go shopping alone?
Who do you usually go shopping with?
How often do you shop online?

5 Speak with Confidence

A *Example conversation*

A: Do you ever buy things on sale?
B: Yes, I often do.
A: [Student writes name.] Thanks. And what do you usually buy?

B *Example conversation*

A: Matthew often buys DVDs on sale. And Francis often buys gifts for friends. Susan does, too.

Lesson 24 Your phone is so cool!

Page 58
1 Vocabulary

A

Answers	
1. light	**5.** slow
2. expensive	**6.** thin
3. small	**7.** narrow
4. dark	**8.** quiet

If it won't confuse students, explain that *light* can mean both *bright* and *not heavy*.

2 Conversation

[CD 2, Track 21]

A

Answers
Iris' phone is light, and it has a cool design.
Iris watches videos on her new phone.

You might want to explain that apps is short for applications and apps are programs you can buy to do more things on smart phones.

Optional Activity

Have students say all the things Iris' phone can do (watch videos, take pictures, play games). Then have them say other things they can do with smart phones (for example, send e-mail, surf the Internet, video chat). Have them practice again using these ideas.

Page 59
3 Language Booster

A

Have students look at the two grammar structures and decide when they use each, providing the answer if necessary. (We use the *be* verb to describe the entire thing, for example, the size or cost. We use *has* or a *has + got* to describe one part of the entire thing, for example, the screen or a function.)

4 Listening

A

[CD 2, Track 22]

Answers		
3	**a.**	(a printer)
2	**b.**	(a video camera)
1	**c.**	(a widescreen TV)
4	**d.**	(MP3 player)

Optional Activity

You might want to have students name each of the electronics. (See answers above in parentheses.)

B

[CD 2, Track 22]

Answers
For each, students should name any two of the following.
1. wide screen, thin, good picture quality
2. nice color (although they don't agree on this), light (weight), small screen, cheap
3. the gray color (for the woman), cheap, makes color copies, heavy (they think that means it is good quality)
4. small, light (weight), white (color), cool design, good price

C Example conversation

A: I look for black MP3 players. They look cool.

B: I like ones that are light and not too expensive.

5 Speak with Confidence

B

You may want to review how to make negative sentences before students do the activity. (For example, Our phone doesn't have a nice camera./ Our phone doesn't.)

Example conversation

A: This phone has a nice camera.

B: Our phone doesn't.

C: Our phone is very light.

D: Ours is, too.

Lessons 21 to 24 Review

English in Action

Page 60

1 Preview

> **Answers**
>
> **Answers will vary.** Sample answer.
> I think the chair is nice. I would pay about $20 for it.

2 Understand

A

> **Answers**
>
> 1. Jill's phone is light and thin.
> 2. Tom doesn't have a brand new phone.
> 3. Eric wants to sell his chair online.
> 4. Eric's chair is not broken./ Eric's chair is in excellent condition.
> 5. Tom buys the chair for $55.

Optional Questions

How often does Jill buy apps for her phone? (She buys them every day.)

Does Jill always pay for the apps? (No, sometimes they are free, and sometimes she pays for them.)

Why is Eric buying a new chair? (He's buying his friend's lucky chair.)

Why does he say it's lucky? (It's lucky because his friend got all As when sitting it while studying.)

3 Discuss

Example conversation

A: Do you think Tom got a good deal?

B: No, I don't. He paid more than a new chair.

A: I agree. How much would you pay?

B: I'd pay $25. How about you?

A: I'd pay $30. What's something you'd like to sell?

B: I'd like to sell my old cell phone because it's heavy and can't send e-mail. I'd sell it for $3.

Speak Now

Page 61

21 *Example conversation*

A: How much is a candy bar?

B: A candy bar is about $1.

A: OK. And how much does a DVD cost?

B: It depends, but many DVDs are about $20.

22 *Example conversation*

B: Will you take $20 for that cell phone?

A: I can give it to you for $40. It's only 6 months old.

B: Will you give it to me for $30?

A: You can have it for $33.

B: OK. That's a good price. Thanks.

23 *Example conversation*

A: Do you ever rent DVDs?

B: No, I never do. I watch movies online.

A: How often do you e-mail?

B: I e-mail eight or ten times a day.

24 *Example conversation*

A: This is my new cell phone. It has some cool apps, and the picture is really good. It's also light.

B: It's great. This is my new tablet computer. It's got a cool design, and it's thin. It's also expensive.

Lesson 25 Do you each much fruit?

Page 62

1 Vocabulary

A

Answers	
meat/protein	**fruit/vegetables**
chicken	carrots
tofu	oranges
nuts	apples
beans	**grains**
dairy	noodles
yogurt	rice
cheese	bread

Optional Activity

You might want to have students name other foods for each category. (For example, Meat/Protein: hamburger, turkey; Dairy: milk, ice cream; Fruit/Vegetables: bananas, broccoli; Grains: pasta)

B *Example conversation*

A: How often do you eat chicken each week?

B: I eat it about twice a week. How often do you eat it?

2 Conversation

[CD 2, Track 23]

A

Answers
Lauren eats nuts for protein. Rob does not eat a lot of vegetables.

Page 63

3 Language Booster

A

- Point out that vegetables has an *s* but fruit does not. Explain that this is because fruit is an uncountable noun.
- Have students look at the questions and decide when to use many and much, providing the answer if necessary. (We use many for things that we cannot count. We use much for things that we can count.)

- Explain that we use an additional word to count uncountable nouns. For example, we can say a glass of water or a liter of water, but we cannot say waters.
- Have students decide whether each food in the Vocabulary section is countable (carrots, oranges, apples) or not (chicken, tofu, yogurt, cheese, rice, bread).
- You might want to explain that some nouns can be both countable and uncountable. For example, a bowl of noodles is uncountable, but each noodle can also be counted. This is also true for nuts and beans.

4 Listening

A

[CD 2, Track 24]

Answers					
	Greg	Emily		Greg	Emily
meat	✗	✓	fruit	✓	✓
fish	✓	✓	vegetables	✓	✗
tofu	✓	✗	ice cream	✗	✓
bread	✓	✓	chocolate	✗	✓

B

[CD 2, Track 24]

Answers
See second column above under Emily.

C

Answers
Answers will vary. Sample answer. I think Greg's eating habits are healthier. He eats healthy food like fruit and vegetables, and he doesn't eat ice cream or chocolate.

Example conversation

A: I think Greg's eating habits are healthier.

B: I think so, too. He doesn't eat ice cream or chocolate. But what's life without chocolate?

5 Speak with Confidence

Example conversation

A: Do you eat many eggs?

B: Yes, I eat them all the time.

[A writes B's name in the chart.]

Lesson 26 We need onions.

Page 64
1 Vocabulary

A

Answers	
Answers will vary. Sample answer.	
an omelet	**pizza**
eggs	olives
onions	flour
salt	tomatoes
pepper	oil
butter	onions

2 Conversation

[CD 2, Track 25]

A

Answers
Ariel is making pizza for dinner.
She needs onions and tomatoes.

Explain that adding *completely (We're completely out)* strengthens the statement. You might want to give a few more examples. (For example, *I'm completely broke* to emphasize the person really has no money right now. *I'm completely exhausted* emphasizes how tired the person is.)

C
[CD 2, Track 26]

Answers
you in the mood for => you craving
We're completely out. => We don't have any.
Yes, we need some. => We have tomatoes.

Page 65
3 Language Booster

A

- If necessary, explain that *what else* suggests something has already been mentioned, so it should not be used to start a discussion.

  Have students decide when to use some and any, providing an explanation, if necessary. (Any is used to ask questions and in negative sentences [i.e., with not]. Some is used in positive sentences.

- Point out that some and any are used in the same way for both count and uncountable nouns.

4 Pronunciation

A
[CD 2, Track 27]

- Explain that this practice focuses on the shortened pronunciation of *What do*. Point out that the o sound in *do* becomes an a sound.

- It may be helpful to have students practice *What do* as a phrase. This should help them combine the two words together more easily.

B

Emphasize that students should use complete sentences.

Example conversation

A: What do we need to make vegetable soup?

B: We need some onion and tomatoes.

A: What do we need at the store?

B: Maybe buy some carrots and potatoes.

A: What do you already have at home?

B: I have tomatoes and vegetable broth.

5 Speak with Confidence

C

Example conversation

A: We are going to make sushi and a salad.

B: We need fish and sushi vinegar. We also need some lettuce.

C: Our group is going to make pizza and cake.

Lesson 27 Do you eat a big lunch?

Page 66
1 Vocabulary

A

> **Answers**
>
> **Answers will vary.** Students should circle the foods they think are healthy, for example:
> salad
> fruit
> chicken
> rice
> vegetables

Optional Activity

If students have different opinions, you may want to have them talk about their reasons for their ideas.

Example conversation

A: I think juice is healthy.

B: It's not always healthy. Some juice has a lot of sugar and not many vitamins.

B

Optional Activity

Have students have conversations about what they eat for lunch and dinner.

2 Conversation

[CD 2, Track 28]

A

> **Answers**
>
> Jae-soon has a small breakfast.
> **Answers will vary.** Sample answer. I don't think Simon has a healthy lunch (because he eats cake and drinks soda).

C

[CD 2, Track 29]

> **Answers**
>
> having => eating
> Is that all you're having? => That's a small lunch.
> like a small breakfast => have a light meal

Page 67
3 Language Booster

B *Example conversation*

A: Do you have a big lunch?

B: No, I don't. I usually have a salad or a sandwich.

4 Pronunciation

A

[CD 2, Track 30]

- Point out that /ɪz/ adds a vowel sound, and as a result, there is another syllable. For example, peach is one syllable, but peaches is two. It may be helpful to have students think of the original word plus *is* until they become used to adding the syllable.

- Explain that /s/ and /z/ do not add a syllable.

- Explain that /ɪz/ is after sounds such as s, z, ks, ch, and c.

B, C

[CD 2, Track 31]

> **Answers**
>
> | /s/ | /ɪz/ |
> | --- | --- |
> | nuts | juices |
> | chips | oranges |
> | carrots | sandwiches |
> | /z/ | |
> | beans | |
> | noodles | |
> | vegetables | |

5 Speak with Confidence

Example conversation

A: Do you prefer an early or a late dinner?

B: I prefer to eat a late dinner.

C: Why?

B: I like to eat after I get home from school, and I don't get home until 8:30.

A: So what time do you eat?

Lesson 28 How does it taste?

Page 68
1 Vocabulary

A

Answers
Answers will vary. Sample answer.

sweet: cake   spicy: taco sauce
bitter: coffee   salty: potato chips
bland: rice   sour: some apples
oily: onion rings

2 Conversation

[CD 2, Track 32]

A

Answers
Rice, seafood, and some spices are in paella. The salad dressing tastes both sweet and sour.

Page 69
3 Language Booster

B

If you think your students may not know some of these foods, bring in pictures (for example, from the Internet) to help them understand them.

Example conversation

A: What's in sushi?

B: Rice with fish, seafood, or egg. How does it taste?

4 Listening

A

[CD 2, Track 33]

Answers
Answers will vary. Sample answer.
4 **a.**
5 **b.**
2 **c.**
1 **d.**
3 **e.**

B

[CD 2, Track 34]

Answers	
1. delicious	4. bland
2. very spicy	5. really sweet
3. really salty	

C Example conversation

A: Which of these foods would you eat?

B: I would eat the soup. I like spicy food. And I would eat the ice cream. I love ice cream. But I wouldn't eat the fish. I don't really like fish. How about you? Which of these foods would you eat?

5 Speak with Confidence

A Example conversation

A: What's a typical dish from your country?

B: Nikujaga.

A: What's in it?

B: It has meat and potatoes, and also some carrots and onions.

A: When do you usually eat it?

B: We often eat it in the winter.

A: How does it taste?

B: It has soy sauce and sugar, so it's a little sweet, I guess.

A: What do you eat with it?

B: We often eat it with rice.

B Example conversation

A: It's a typical dish from my country. It has meat, potatoes, carrots, and onions. We often eat it in the winter. It has soy sauce and sugar, so it's a little sweet. We eat it with rice. What is it?

B: Is it nikujaga?

A: That's right.

Lessons 25 to 28 Review

English in Action

Page 70

1 Preview

> **Answers**
>
> **Answers will vary.** Sample answer.
> I see bread, broccoli, and tomatoes (also, potatoes, an apple, and milk). You can make a salad or maybe a sandwich.

2 Understand

A

> **Answers**
>
> 1. potatoes
> 2. onions
> 3. carrots
> 4. coconut milk
> 5. rice
> 6. lots of spices

B

> **Answers**
>
> 1. wants to try something new
> 2. eats a lot of vegetables
> 3. don't like to eat potatoes
> 4. makes pasta

Optional Questions

Why doesn't Eric want pasta for dinner? (They have had pasta every day for the past few weeks.)

Why do they decide not to make curry? (They need to buy most of the ingredients but don't have time to go to the supermarket.)

How does Tom describe his pasta? (He says it's not too salty and not too sweet, and he says it's delicious.)

3 Discuss

Example conversation

A: How often do you shop for food?

B: I don't like to shop, so I only shop for food once a week.

A: What's something you cook well?

B: Every time I make a cake, everyone says it's really good.

A: I'd like to try your cake. So, which three items would you choose from the Preview section?

B: I'd choose the jam, the bread, an apple, and the broccoli and then I'd make a jam sandwich and have a broccoli salad and an apple with it. So how about you? How often do you shop for food?

Speak Now

Page 71

25 *Example conversation*

A: Do you eat much cheese?

B: Yes, I love cheese. I eat it about five times a week.

A: OK. And do you eat a lot of fruit?

B: No, I don't. It's really expensive.

26 *Example conversation*

A: What do you want to make for dinner tonight?

B: I want to make soup.

A: What do you need to buy?

B: I need some onions, meat, potatoes, and celery.

27 *Example conversation*

A: I eat eggs and toast for breakfast. I love soup and a small sandwich for lunch. I like to have Mexican food for dinner.

B: What kind of sandwich do you like?

A: I like egg salad sandwiches.

B: And how do you eat your eggs?

A: I fry them.

B: Soup and a sandwich are probably healthy, but Mexican food has a lot of fat and calories. Your breakfast might be healthy, but you should eat more fruits and vegetables.

28 *Example conversation*

A: I love burritos.

B: What are the ingredients?

A: Beef, cheese, sour cream, and refried beans.

B: How does it taste?

Lesson 29 I had a great weekend.

Page 72
1 Vocabulary

A

Answers
Answers will vary. Sample answer.

didn't study	went shopping
didn't stay home	saw a movie
met friends	got a haircut

Optional Activity

You might want to have students say things they did and didn't do last weekend. (For example, didn't visit relatives, did homework, worked)

2 Conversation

[CD 2, Track 35]

A

Answers
Jun had a great weekend.
Erica stayed home and studied for the history test.

Page 73
3 Language Booster

A

Point out that students should only use one past tense verb. If they did the activity, the action verb is said in the past tense. However, if they didn't do the activity, they should use *didn't* (which is past tense) and the present tense verb showing the action.

B

Example conversation

A: How was your weekend?

B: I had a great weekend.

A: What did you do?

B: I met some friends on Friday night. We watched a movie. On Saturday I went shopping. On Sunday I didn't do anything special.

4 Listening

A

[CD 2, Track 36]

Answers	
1. great	**2.** so-so

B

[CD 2, Track 36]

Answers	
Tom	**Andrea**
watched sports	watched sports ✓
played sports ✓	played sports
went shopping	went shopping ✓
went to a restaurant ✓	went to a restaurant ✓
watched TV ✓	watched TV ✓

C

Example conversation

A: Did you watch sports?

B: No, I didn't, but I played sports. I played baseball. I also went shopping and went to a restaurant, but I didn't watch TV. How about you? What did you do this past weekend?

5 Speak with Confidence

A

Answers
Answers will vary. Sample answer.
watched TV
went shopping
did my homework
went to the movies

B

Example conversation

A: How was your weekend?

B: It was great.

C: What did you do?

A: On Saturday I went to the movies.

D: Who did you go with?

A: Sansfica and Noel.

C: What else did you do?

Lesson 30 What time did you call?

Page 74

1 Vocabulary

A

Answers	
2 last month	**6** yesterday afternoon
5 yesterday morning	**3** last week
1 last year	**4** the day before yesterday
7 last night	**8** this morning

B

Answers
1. a movie last week
2. my grandmother last night
3. to a nice restaurant last month
4. a delicious chicken burger with my friends the day before yesterday

2 Conversation

[CD 2, Track 37]

A

Answers
Last night Sarah went to a movie.
Last night Terry did his homework.

C

[CD 2, Track 38]

Answers
What time => When
between 9:00 and 10:00 => around 9:30
Did you finish it? => Are you done?

Page 75

3 Language Booster

A

Point out that we use one past tense verb in each question (i.e., did, were, did) and that other verbs in the questions are present tense (i.e., finish, do).

B *Example conversation*

A: Did you watch TV yesterday?

B: No, I didn't. Did you?

A: Yes, I did. Where did you go after your last English class?

B: I went to my part-time job. How about you?

4 Pronunciation

A

[CD 2, Track 39]

B

[CD 2, Track 40]

Answers		
/t/	/d/	/ɪd/
finished	played	waited
skipped	turned	started
worked	stayed	wanted

C *Example conversation*

A: I finished my homework last night.

B: I didn't skip class. I never skip class.

A: I worked at a fast-food restaurant last year.

B: I played tennis in junior high school.

A: I turned 21 last week.

B: I stayed home last night.

A: I waited for my sister this morning. She's always late.

B: I started reading this book the day before yesterday.

A: I wanted to watch a movie yesterday, but I didn't.

5 Speak with Confidence

Remind students to practice eye contact while talking.

Lesson 31 You won't believe this!

Page 76
1 Vocabulary

A

Answers	
N scary	P fantastic
P amazing	N terrible
N awful	P exciting
N dangerous	P incredible

2 Conversation

[CD 2, Track 41]

A

Answers
David learned to scuba dive. He says the shark was small and not dangerous.

C

[CD 2, Track 42]

Answers
It was awesome! => I had the best time! you won't believe => you'll never guess you'll never guess what happened => listen to this

Page 77
3 Language Booster

B

Answers
Answers will vary. Sample answer.
a famous movie star   a new coat leg   passport

Example conversation

A: You won't believe this. I lost my passport on vacation.

B: That's terrible! You'll never guess what happened to me. I saw a famous movie star on the street this morning.

A: That's fantastic! Who did you see?

4 Listening

A

[CD 2, Track 43]

Answers
4 **a.**
3 **b.**
2 **c.**
1 **d.**

B

[CD 2, Track 43]

Answers	
1. How awful!	**3.** How terrible.
2. That's exciting!	**4.** That's fantastic!

C *Example conversation*

A: Does Donna's vacation sound good to you?

B: Yes, it does. I'd love to try cooking Thai food, and it would be fun to try riding on an elephant. How about you? Does her vacation sound good to you?

5 Speak with Confidence

A

Answers
Answers will vary. Sample answer. I went to Vietnam. I went shopping and went to some markets. I went last summer. I loved the food. I went with two friends, and we met another friend there. I didn't like the rain. It rained several days.

B *Example conversation*

A: So, where did you go?

B: I went to Vietnam.

C: That's incredible! Who did you go with?

A: I went with two friends, and we met another friend there.

D: That's fantastic! What did you do there?

A: I went shopping and went to some markets.

Lesson 32 What are your plans?

Page 78
1 Vocabulary

A

Answers
Answers will vary. Sample answer.

__ prepare for a test	__ stay up late
✓ go to the mall	__ go out of town
✓ watch sports	__ go to a park
✓ visit relatives	__ go to a museum

2 Conversation

[CD 2, Track 44]

A

Answers
Mark and Reid are going to watch the tennis finals. Reid and Alan are going to go to the science museum together. They are going to look at the new robots display.

Page 79
3 Language Booster

A

You might want to teach the response *I haven't decided yet.*

B Example conversation

A: What are you doing after class?

B: I'm going to go to the cafeteria to eat lunch. What are your plans for tonight?

4 Pronunciation

A

[CD 2, Track 45]

- You might want to explain that even though they combine the words going and to, they should not add another *to* (i.e., they should not say *gonna to*).

- Remind students that they must still include the *be* verb (for example, *am* in I am/I'm).

- Tell students that when they say *gonna* the *o* sounds less like an *o* and more like the schwa.

- You might want to tell students that *want to* is reduced in a similar way.

B Example conversation

A: What are you gonna do this weekend?

B: I'm gonna go to the museum. What are you gonna do this weekend?

A: I'm gonna work at my part-time job at a fast-food restaurant.

B: What are you gonna do after work?

A: I'm gonna go home and take a shower. I always smell like hamburgers and chicken after work.

B: When are you gonna start work on Saturday?

A: I'm gonna start at 9:00. What about you? Are you gonna work this Saturday?

B: No, but I'm gonna work on Sunday.

A: How many hours are you gonna work?

B: I'm gonna work 8 hours. I work 8 hours every weekend.

5 Speak with Confidence

A

Answers
Answers will vary. Sample answer.
work
sleep in late

B Example conversation

A: Are you gonna work this weekend?

B: Yes, I am.

C Example conversation

A: Nigel is gonna work this weekend.

B: So is Nathan.

C: Natsuki is gonna go shopping.

D: So is Carol, and Don is gonna go out of town.

Lessons 29 to 32 Review

English in Action

Page 80

1 Preview

> **Answers**
>
> **Answers will vary.** Sample answer.
> I think Jill visited Washington, D.C.

2 Understand

A

> **Answers**
>
> **a.** (Jill is telling Eric about her vacation in this picture.)
> **b.** 1
> **c.** 3
> **d.** 2

B

> **Answers**
>
> Students should circle the following verbs.
>
> be (was)   see (saw)
> decide (decided)   start (started)
> get (got)   take (took)
> change (changed)   play (played)
> go (went)   escape (escaped)

Optional

Have students listen again and write down the past tense verbs. (Answers in parentheses above.)

Optional Questions

How much was the video camera? (It was $175.)

Where did Eric see dinosaurs? (At an exhibition at the Smithsonian. / At a museum.)

3 Discuss

Example conversation

A: Yesterday I went shopping, saw a movie, and worked at my part-time job.

B: I don't think you watched a movie.

A: You're right. So, are you going to continue to study English?

B: Yes, of course. I love English. How about you?

Speak Now

Page 81

29 *Example conversation*

A: On Saturday and Sunday I went out for lunch. I didn't go shopping, and I didn't work. I went to a movie on Sunday afternoon.

B: Wow! I think you had a great weekend.

30 *Example conversation*

A: Last month I took a trip to China.

B: Really? Who did you go with?

A: I went with my classmates.

B: Where did you go?

A: We went to Ningxia and Xian.

B: Why did you go to Ningxia?

A: Our school has an exchange with the university there.

B: How long did you stay in Ningxia?

A: We stayed for about five days.

B: Did you see the terracotta warriors in Xian?

A: Yes, we did. They were amazing!

31 *Example conversation*

A: Listen to this! Last night I saw that new movie—a week before it is released!

B: That's fantastic! How was it?

32 *Example conversation*

A: What are your plans for the weekend?

B: I'm going to go to a baseball game.

A: Who's playing?

B: The Mariners.

A: Who are you going to go with?

B: Thomas and Lee. Do you want to come?

1 How are you?

Part 1

Complete the conversation with your own answers. In class, practice the conversations with a partner.

New teacher: Hi! What's your first name?

You: _____

New teacher: And what's your last name?

You: _____

New teacher: What's your middle name?

You: _____

New teacher: Great. Thanks. It's nice to meet you.

Part 2

Choose the best word or phrase to complete each conversation. In class, practice the conversations with a partner.

1.

Yuko: (Hi, Mao. / How are you doing, Mao?)
Mao: Fine, thanks.
Yuko: Oh, my train is here.
Mao: (Fine, thanks. / OK. Good night.)

2.

Ms. Anders: (Hey / Hello), Ms. Kim.
Ms. Kim: How is everything?
Ms. Anders: Everything is great, thank you. How are you?
Ms. Kim: (Good. / I'm fine, thank you.)

3.

Francis: Hi, Andy. How are things?
Andy: I'm all right. You?
Francis: (Not bad. / I'm fine, thank you.)

4.

Melissa: (Good night / Goodbye), Professor Ramos.
Ms. Ramos: Goodbye, Melissa.

2 Nice to meet you.

Part 1

Match the words from the box to their definitions.

| classmate | teacher | friend | neighbor | relative | colleague | boss | stranger |

1. A person you work with is a _____.
2. Someone you don't know at all is a _____.
3. Someone who lives near you is a _____.
4. One of the people you study with is a _____.
5. The person who tells you what to do at your job is your _____.
6. The person who helps you learn in class is your _____.
7. A person such as your mother's mother is a _____.
8. Someone you like to spend time with is a _____.

Part 2

How often do you see the people in Part 1? Put them in order from most often to least often. In class, talk about your ideas with a partner.

_____

_____

Part 3

Write the words from Part 1 to complete the first sentence in each conversation. Then write what the second person says. In class, practice the conversations with a partner.

1.

Yukiko: Excuse me, Ralph. This is my _____. We work together at Oxford University Press.

Ralph: _____.

2.

YeQuing: Hi, Bak. I'd like you to meet my _____. We first met 10 years ago.

Bak: _____.

3.

Inger: Hi. I'm Inger, and this is my _____. I live in 4A, and he lives in 5B.

David: _____.

Lesson 2   **43**

3 Can you say that again?

Part 1

Write one or two words to complete each way of communicating. If a word is not needed, write an X.

1. _____ an e-mail

2. _____ a text

3. _____ in person

4. _____ instant message

5. _____ video chat

6. _____ social network

7. _____ a letter

8. _____ on the phone

Part 2

Do you do each activity in Part 1 alone, with another person, or sometimes alone and sometimes with another person? Write each activity in the correct place in the diagram.

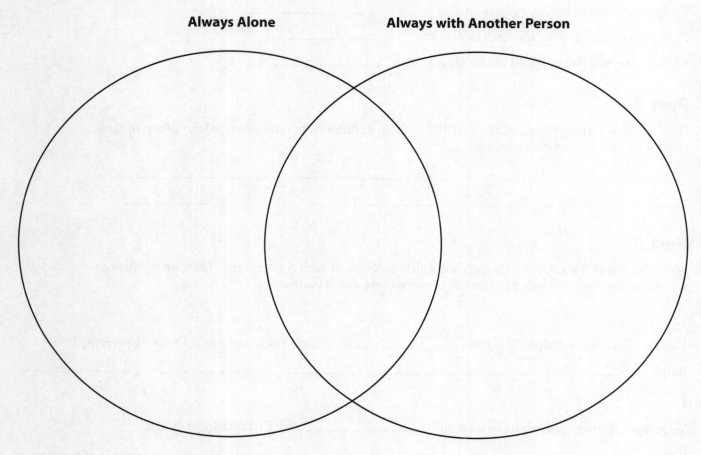

Always Alone   **Always with Another Person**

In class, compare answers with a partner.

A: I usually write an e-mail alone. How about you?

B: I do, too.

4 Nice weather, isn't it?

Part 1

How often do you talk about these things? Put them in order from 1 (most often) to 8 (least often, never). Who do you talk with? Write your answer on the second line.

In class, talk about your ideas with a partner.

_____ school _____   _____ movies _____

_____ family _____   _____ hobbies _____

_____ music _____   _____ money _____

_____ sports _____   _____ TV shows _____

Part 2

Check (✓) the sentences and questions you might use to make small talk.

_____ It's really beautiful today, isn't it?

_____ It really is.

_____ This sunny weather is great, isn't it?

_____ How old are you?

_____ Yeah, this cloudy weather sure is terrible.

_____ How's school/work?

_____ Hot/cold, huh?

_____ What's your middle name?

_____ I'm really busy these days. You?

Part 3

Use some of the sentences and questions in Part 2 to make two short conversations. Practice them with a partner in class.

1.

You: _____

Partner: _____

2.

You: _____

Partner: _____

5 I love hip-hop!

Part 1

Do you like this music? Write I love [the music] (☺☺), I like [the music] (☺), I don't really like [the music] (☹), or I don't like [the music] at all (☹☹).

1. rock _____ I don't really like rock. _____
2. pop _____
3. country _____
4. hip-hop _____
5. classical _____
6. jazz _____
7. folk _____
8. techno _____
9. heavy metal _____
10. reggae _____

In class, compare answers with a partner. Do you like the same music or different music?

A: I don't really like rock music. Do you?

B: I love it!

Part 2

In each of B's answers, one word is wrong. Cross it out and write the correct word on the line. In class, practice the correct conversations with your partner.

1. **A:** I love techno.

   B: Really? I ~~do.~~ _____don't_____

2. **A:** I don't like jazz at all.

   B: Either do I. _____

3. **A:** I like reggae.

   B: Me neither. _____

4. **A:** I really like country.

   B: Neither do I. _____

5. **A:** I don't really like hip-hop.

   B: Oh, I don't. _____

6. **A:** I really dislike heavy metal.

   B: Really? I do. _____

Part 3

Look at the conversations in Part 2. Do A and B like the same (S) music or different (D) music?

1. _____
2. _____
3. _____
4. _____
5. _____
6. _____

6 My favorite movie is…

Part 1

Rank these interests from 1 (most interesting for you) to 8 (not at all interesting to you). Then write three words about that interest.

In class, talk about your ideas with a partner.

1. _____ movies
   _____ actor, actress, Emma Watson _____

2. _____ sports
   _____

3. _____ food
   _____

4. _____ video games
   _____

5. _____ music
   _____

6. _____ books
   _____

7. _____ shopping
   _____

8. _____ travel
   _____

Part 2

Use your ideas from Part 1 and other ideas to complete the conversation. In class, get into groups of three and practice it.

You: What's your favorite movie?

Partner 1: **1.** _____ My favorite movie is _____.

Partner 2: I like **2.** _____.

Partner 1: How about actors and actresses? Who's your favorite actress?

You: I'm crazy about **3.** _____.

Partner 1: Really? **4.** _____.

Partner 2: And what about music? What's your favorite song?

You: **5.** _____.

Partner 2: So you like **6.** _____?

You: **7.** _____.

Partner 1: Well, what about video games? Do you like any games in particular?

You: **8.** _____.

Lesson 6 **47**

7 What time is it?

Part 1

What time is it? Draw clocks.

It's half past eleven.

It's five to four.

It's a quarter after one.

It's a quarter to nine.

It's noon.

It's midnight.

Part 2

What time is it? Write your answers in words. Use *after* and *to*.

1. 10:05 _____ .
2. 3:10 _____ .
3. 8:20 _____ .
4. 6:25 _____ .
5. 7:40 _____ .
6. 5:50 _____ .
7. 1:35 _____ .

Part 3

Look at your schedule. Answer the questions using words.

Monday	
10:30	English class
1:00	Work
7:30	Birthday party

1. What time is your English class? _____
2. What time is your job? _____
3. What time is the birthday party? _____

8 Would you try kayaking?

Part 1

Which word is different? Circle it. In class, talk about why it is different with a partner.

1. dangerous   hard   (golf)
2. soccer   baseball   bungee jumping
3. kayaking   interesting   challenging
4. rock climbing   skydiving   wrestling
5. exciting   boring   fun
6. snowboarding   skateboarding   boxing
7. surfing   jet skiing   soccer

Part 2

Complete the conversation with your own answers. Practice it with a partner in class.

Friend: What do you think about jet skiing?

You: I think it's _____.

Friend: Really? I think _____.

Part 3

Use the words from Part 1 to write the opposites.

exciting   _____   safe   _____   easy   _____

Part 4

Do you use a ball to do the activities in Part 1? Do you do them inside? Are they dangerous? Write the activities in the diagram below. In class, compare answers with a partner.

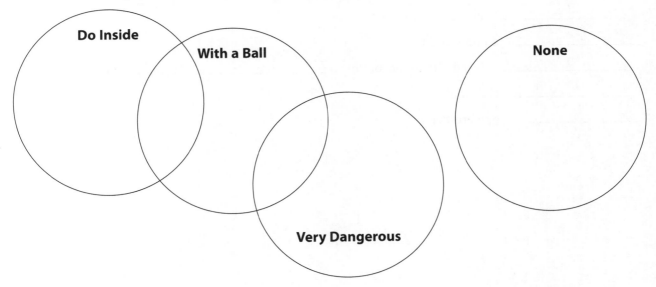

Lesson 8   **49**

9 Do you have any brothers?

Part 1

A family tree shows all of the people in a family. Imagine this is part of your father's family tree. Write the words to finish the tree.

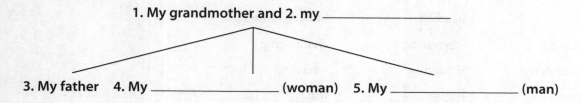

1. My grandmother and 2. my _____

3. My father   4. My _____ **(woman)   5. My** _____ **(man)**

Part 2

Look at the family tree in Part 1. Complete the sentences.

1. Person 1 and person 2 are my _____.
2. Person 4's daughter is my _____.
3. Person 5's son is my _____.
4. Person 5's son is my father's _____.
5. Person 4's daughter is my father's _____.
6. My mother and father are my _____.

Part 3

Complete the sentences with true information about you. In class, take turns reading your sentences with a partner.

1. I _____ two sisters.
2. My _____ is single.
3. My _____ is married.
4. My _____ is _____ years old.
5. I _____ an only child.
6. My _____ is older than me, but my _____ is younger than me.
7. I _____ children.
8. I _____ one brother.

10 She's pretty smart.

Part 1

Are these personalities positive, negative, or both? In class, talk about your ideas with a partner.

| serious | shy | patient | smart | funny | quiet | friendly | confident |

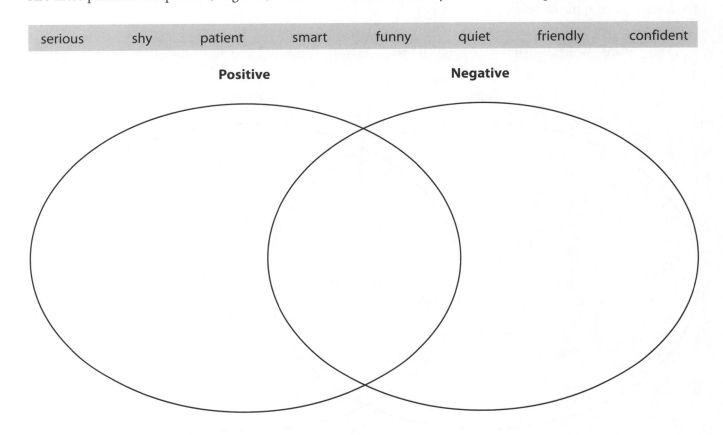

Positive **Negative**

Part 2

Use the words from Part 1 to complete each sentence. You won't use one word.

1. You and your friend waited in a long line for 30 minutes. Your friend wasn't angry.
   She is _____.

2. While you waited in line, your friend talked to many people. She is also _____.

3. It was fun waiting with your friend, but you can't talk to other people very easily. You are kind of quiet
   and _____.

4. Your friend is good at studying English. He is very _____ and got an A on his last English test.

5. Your friend always thinks he will do well. People think he is _____.

6. Many people smile when your friend says interesting things. He is _____.

7. You always think a lot before you do things. You are _____.

Part 3

1. Think about you and your friend. Which sentences in Part 2 are true? _____

2. Which sentences aren't true? _____

11 I love your shirt!

Part 1

Are these clothes tops (things you wear on the top part of your body), bottoms, or both? Write them in the correct place in the diagram.

| jackets   jeans   shirts   T-shirts   shorts   skirts   sweaters   dresses   watches   bracelets   rings   belts |

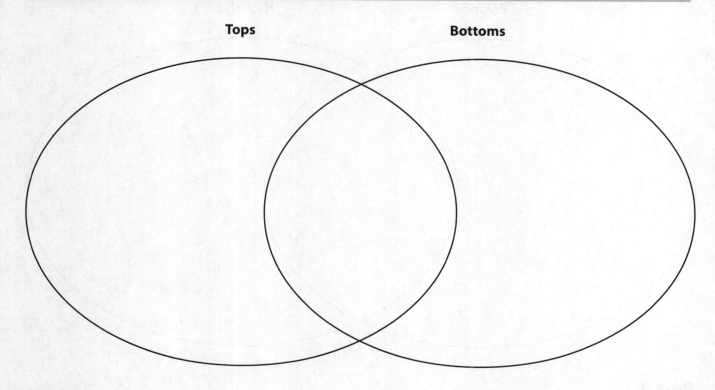

Tops   Bottoms

Part 2

Add three more kinds of clothes to the diagram in Part 1. In class, compare your ideas with a partner.

Part 3

Complete the sentences with words from Part 1. In class, talk about your ideas with a partner.

1. People wear _____ and _____ when it's cold.

2. People wear _____ and _____ when it's hot.

3. People wear _____ so they know what time it is.

4. People often wear _____ when they are married.

5. People often wear _____ to keep their jeans up.

6. Usually only women wear _____ and _____ .

12 What's she wearing?

Part 1

Find the 11 color words in the puzzle below. The words go

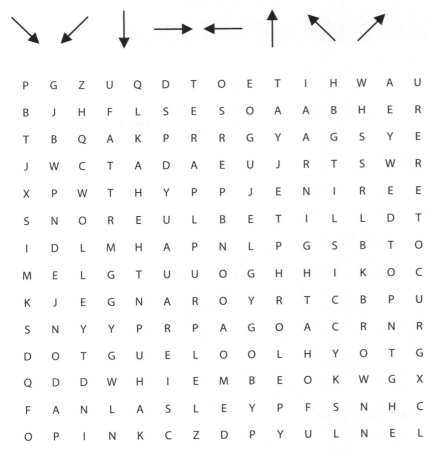

P	G	Z	U	Q	D	T	O	E	T	I	H	W	A	U
B	J	H	F	L	S	E	S	O	A	A	B	H	E	R
T	B	Q	A	K	P	R	R	G	Y	A	G	S	Y	E
J	W	C	T	A	D	A	E	U	J	R	T	S	W	R
X	P	W	T	H	Y	P	P	J	E	N	I	R	E	E
S	N	O	R	E	U	L	B	E	T	I	L	L	D	T
I	D	L	M	H	A	P	N	L	P	G	S	B	T	O
M	E	L	G	T	U	U	O	G	H	H	I	K	O	C
K	J	E	G	N	A	R	O	Y	R	T	C	B	P	U
S	N	Y	Y	P	R	P	A	G	O	A	C	R	N	R
D	O	T	G	U	E	L	O	O	L	H	Y	O	T	G
Q	D	D	W	H	I	E	M	B	E	O	K	W	G	X
F	A	N	L	A	S	L	E	Y	P	F	S	N	H	C
O	P	I	N	K	C	Z	D	P	Y	U	L	N	E	L

Part 2

Look at the letters you didn't circle. Write every 6th letter below to find the hidden message.

__ _T_ __ _H_ __ __ __ __ __   __ __ __ __

__ __ __ __ __ __ __ __   __ __ __ __ __ __ __ __

__ __ __ __ __ __   __ __ __   __ __ __ __ __ .

Part 3

Write sentences with three of the colors. In class, take turns reading them with a partner.

1. _____

2. _____

3. _____

Lesson 12   **53**

13 When do you get up?

Part 1

When do you usually do these activities? Write them in the correct place in the diagram.

| check e-mail | watch TV | talk on the phone | study | take a shower | exercise |

Mornings

Never

Afternoons

Evenings

Part 2

Add three more activities to the diagram in Part 1. In class, compare your ideas with a partner.

Part 3

Answer the questions so they are true for you. In class, take turns asking and answering the questions with a partner.

1. On the days when you get up early, what time do you wake up? _____

2. When do you usually have lunch? _____

3. What time do you usually get home on Wednesdays? _____

4. What time do you usually eat dinner on Fridays? _____

5. When do you usually go to bed? _____

6. What time do you get to class on Thursday? _____

7. Do you usually talk on the phone every day? _____

14 When do you get there?

Part 1

Write one or two words to complete each activity. If a word is not needed, write an X.

1. _____ shopping
2. _____ work out
3. _____ the mall
4. _____ movies

5. _____ to eat
6. _____ to the library
7. _____ sports
8. _____ walk

Part 2

How often do you do the activities in Part 1? Put the activities in order from most often to least often. In class, talk about your ideas with a partner.

_____

_____

Part 3

Write the activities from Part 1 to complete the first sentence in each conversation. Write a follow-up question for the second person in each conversation. In class, practice the conversations with a partner.

1.

Lian: I love to _____.

Anna: _____ When _____?

2.

Eduardo: I _____ every day.

Keiko: _____?

3.

Maria: I usually _____ alone.

Manuel: _____?

4.

Andrew: I usually _____ with my friends.

Matteo: _____?

15 What do you do first?

Part 1

When do you do these activities? Put the words into the best column for you. In class, talk about your ideas with a partner.

| go out with friends | sleep in late | don't do much | get up early |
| feel my best | stay up late | feel my worst | |

Saturday-Sunday	Monday-Friday	Never
_____	_____	_____
_____	_____	_____
_____	_____	_____
_____	_____	_____
_____	_____	_____

Part 2

Write each of the activities from Part 1 once to complete the story.

My name is Maria. During the week, I usually get up at 6:45, but yesterday I got up at 5:30. I don't usually

(1) _____ like that. On Saturday night I usually (2) _____.

We go out to eat or go to movies. I usually don't get home until after midnight. I don't really like to

(3) _____ like that because the next day it's hard to get up. Because we stay out late,

I usually (4) _____ on Sunday. Sometimes I get up at 11:00! When I do that, I

(5) _____, and I especially don't study or work. I just watch TV and go shopping. My

friends say, "I love Friday. I (6) _____ on Friday because the weekend is about to start."

I (7) _____ on Sunday. I like to get up and go to bed at the same time every day.

Part 3

Answer the questions. In class, compare answers with a partner.

1. When you sleep in late, what time do you get up? _____.

2. What time do you go to bed when you stay up late? _____.

3. What do you do on days when you don't do much? _____.

4. When you go out with friends, what do you usually do? _____.

5. What do you do first after you get up? _____.

6. What do you usually do after lunch? _____.

7. What do you usually do after dinner? _____.

8. What time do you usually have breakfast? _____.

9. What do you do after that? _____.

16 What are you doing?

Part 1

Complete the sentences with class names.

1. Young children study 1+1=2 in _____ classes.

2. _____ is the study of how people think.

3. You study how to run companies when you study _____.

4. People who like to read sometimes study _____ in college.

5. _____ is the study of how groups of people act together.

6. People who like numbers and think about what they mean like _____.

7. If you know a lot about what happened 200 years ago, you know a lot about _____.

8. You have to know _____ to sell things.

9. _____ includes things related to money, including how to make, buy, and sell things.

10. Around the world, _____ is a popular language to study.

Part 2

Answer the questions. In class, compare your answers with a partner.

1. Which of the classes in Part 1 are you taking these days? _____

2. Which of those classes do you love? _____

3. Which do you not really like? _____

Part 3

What kind of people like taking the classes in Part 1? Choose seven more classes. Write the class and one or two characteristics for each person. In class, talk about your ideas with a partner.

<u>English: like to talk with people from other countries</u> _____

_____

_____

_____

_____

_____

_____

_____

17 What's your place like?

Part 1

Write the room that matches the definition.

1. _____ this room in homes often has a TV
2. _____ the room in homes where people eat
3. _____ the room in some houses where you wash your clothes
4. _____ the room in apartments where people usually sleep
5. _____ the place outside and near homes, often with grass, trees, and/or flowers
6. _____ the room in an apartment where you can take a shower
7. _____ the room in your apartment where you cook

Part 2

Which rooms in Part 1 do you have in your place?

_____

In class, compare answers with a partner.

Part 3

How much time do you spend in the rooms in Part 2? Put them in order from the most time to the least time.

_____

_____

Part 4

Use the words below to write about your place or your English classroom. In class, takes turns reading your sentences with a partner.

big	comfortable	convenient	noisy	quiet	small

_____

_____

_____

_____

_____

_____

18 Where can I get a lamp?

Read the hints and write the words to complete the crossword puzzle.

Across

3. It keeps food cold in the summer.
4. It washes the dishes.
5. You open the door and put things in it.
6. You sit on them.
8. You sleep on it.
9. You put clothes in it.
10. You cook on it.
12. Two or three people can sit on it in the living room.

Down

1. They help you see at night.
2. A short table, usually in the living room.
7. You put things on them. They're on walls.
11. You can watch the news on it.

Part 1

Match the places on the left with their definitions on the right.

1. bank
2. drugstore
3. hair salon
4. movie theater
5. department store
6. mall
7. library
8. post office

A. a place where you can buy many different things

B. a place where you go to watch films

C. a big building with many small stores inside

D. a place where you get and keep your money

E. a place where you buy things to help you when you are sick

F. a place where you can send a letter

G. a place women go to get their hair cut

H. a place where you can read books and magazines

Part 2

Complete the sentences with information that is true for you. In class, take turns reading your sentences with a partner.

1. _____ is the best movie theater for seeing movies.

2. A department store _____ the best place to shop for clothes.

3. The nearest library is _____.

4. At the mall, I like to hang out with friends at _____.

5. There is a good hair salon _____.

6. The _____ is near the bank.

7. Many people go to _____
   because it's the _____ drugstore.

8. The nearest post office is _____.

20 Take a left.

Read the conversations. What place are they talking about? Write your answer on the line. In class, practice the conversations with a partner.

1. _____

A: Hi. Do you want to go to a baseball game on Sunday?

B: Sounds great!

2. _____

Mom: It's a beautiful day. Why don't you go out to play?

Son: There's a soccer game on the field, and I'm too old for the other things there.

3. _____

Driver: Where to?

A: The Carlton Hotel, please.

4. _____

A: Excuse me. Does this one go to Pennsylvania Avenue?

B: No, but the next bus does. It's number 17A.

5. _____

Announcement: Next stop, Diamond Hill. Change here for the East Kowloon Line.

6. _____

Radio announcer: The cars on I-105 aren't moving at all. You should take another road unless you like sitting in your car and listening to the radio for a long time!

7. _____

A: Do you want to go fishing at 2:00?

B: Sure. I'll meet you there.

8. _____

News reporter: Last night, some trees fell over it, so cars on Highway 26 can't cross the river this morning.

Lesson 20   **61**

21 How much is coffee?

Part 1

Rank these things from 1 (the most expensive) to 6 (the least expensive).

_____ a haircut   _____ bus fare

_____ a cup of coffee   _____ a taxi ride across town

_____ a movie ticket   _____ museum admission fee

Part 2

Use your ideas from Part 1 to complete the conversations. You can use some things more than once. In class, practice the conversations with a partner.

1.

A: Museum admission fees are _____ than movie tickets.

B: I know. _____ are too expensive for me.

2.

A: I think _____ is reasonable.

B: Me, too. But it also depends on the place. At _____, _____ costs
_____, but at _____ it costs _____.

3.

A: _____ can cost _____!

B: Yeah, but the cost depends on where you go.

4.

A: I think _____
costs the least, and _____ costs the most.

B: I think it depends. _____ is
usually more expensive than _____,
but sometimes _____ is even more expensive!

Part 3

How often do you pay for the things in Part 1? Write them in order from the most often to the least often (never). In class, talk about your ideas with a partner.

_____

_____

_____

_____

22 Will you take $20?

Part 1

For each thing, write three examples.

1. clothes _____ *pants, shorts, a sweater* _____
2. makeup _____
3. toys _____
4. sports equipment _____
5. electronics _____
6. furniture _____
7. CDs _____
8. video games _____

In class, compare answers with a partner.

A: Pants, shorts, and a sweater are examples of clothes.

B: Yeah. And so are jeans, a jacket, and a T-shirt.

Part 2

What do you think about each of the things in Part 1? Put them in the diagram. In class, with your partner talk about why you put each one where you did.

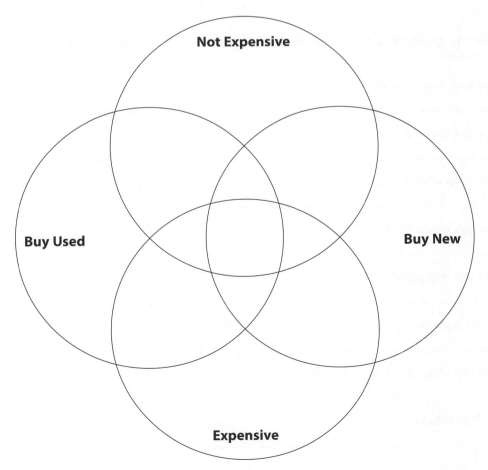

23 Do you ever buy books?

Part 1

How do you buy these things? Put them in the diagram. In class, with your partner talk about why you put each one where you did.

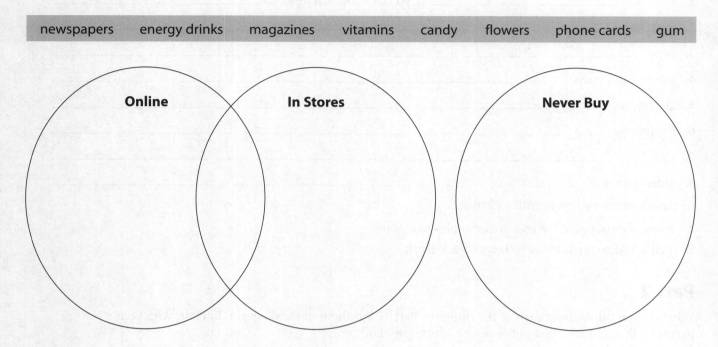

newspapers   energy drinks   magazines   vitamins   candy   flowers   phone cards   gum

Online   In Stores   Never Buy

Part 2

Answer the questions, giving reasons when you can. In class, take turns asking and answering the questions with a partner.

1. How often do you shop for clothes?
   _____.

2. When do you get flowers?
   _____.

3. What kind of magazines do you read?
   _____.

4. When do you buy used comic books?
   _____.

5. How often do you buy gum?
   _____.

6. Do you ever use a phone card?
   _____.

7. How often do you read newspapers on the Internet?
   _____.

8. Do you often buy candy?
   _____.

24 Your phone is so cool!

Part 1

Which word is different? Circle it. In class, with a partner talk about why it is different.

1. heavy	(thick)	light
2. fast	slow	thin
3. quiet	cheap	expensive
4. noisy	quiet	wide
5. dark	narrow	wide
6. thin	thick	bright
7. small	noisy	large
8. dark	narrow	bright

Part 2

What can you describe with the words in Part 1? Put them in the diagram. In class, with your partner talk about why you put each one where you did.

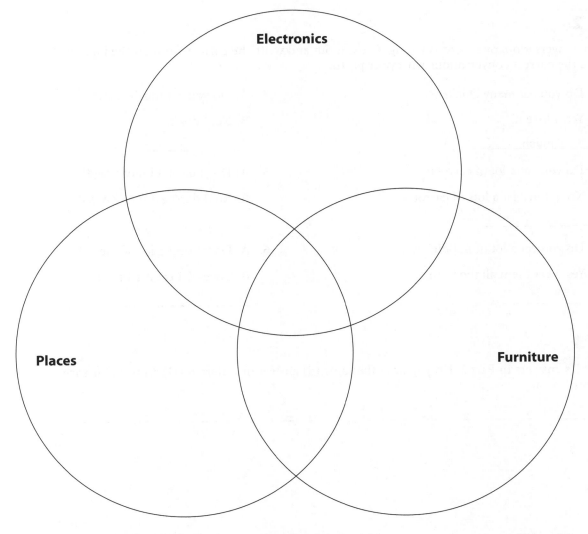

25 Do you eat much fruit?

Part 1

How often do you eat these foods? Put the words into the best column for you. In class, talk about your ideas with a partner.

| chicken | yogurt | tofu | carrots | noodles | oranges | nuts | rice | apples | beans | bread | cheese |

A lot	Not many/much	Never
_____	_____	_____
_____	_____	_____
_____	_____	_____
_____	_____	_____
_____	_____	_____
_____	_____	_____
_____	_____	_____

Part 2

In each conversation, one word is wrong. Cross it out and write the correct word on the line. In class, practice the correct conversations with your partner.

1. **A:** Do you eat ~~many~~ chicken?

   B: Yes, I love it.

   _____much_____

2. **A:** Do you eat a lot of carrots?

   B: No, I don't eat a lots of carrots.

   _____

3. **A:** Do you eat a lot of noodle?

   B: Yes, I eat them all the time.

   _____

4. **A:** Do you eat much rices?

   B: No, I don't.

   _____

5. **A:** Do you eat a lot of bread?

   B: No, I don't eat many bread.

   _____

6. **A:** Do you eat a lot of cheese?

   B: Cheese? I eat it all the times.

   _____

Part 3

Look at B's answers in Part 2. Do you have the same (S) answer or different (D) answers for each question?

1. _____ 2. _____ 3. _____ 4. _____ 5. _____ 6. _____

26 We need onions.

Part 1

Look at the first part of the recipes for two dishes. Put the words below into the correct column.

| butter | salt | oil | tomatoes | flour | onions | pepper | eggs | olives |

In neither	In both	In only one
_____	_____	_____
_____	_____	_____
_____	_____	_____
_____	_____	_____
_____	_____	_____
_____	_____	_____

Chocolate Chip Cookies
1 C. butter
1 1/2 C. sugar
2 eggs
2 t. vanilla
2 C. flour
2/3 C. cocoa powder
3/4 t. baking soda
1/4 t. salt
2 C. chocolate chips

Spanish Potato Omelet
1/2 C. oil
4 potatoes
Little salt
Little pepper
1 large onion
4 eggs
2 tomatoes

Part 2

1. Think about one of your favorite dishes. What is it?

   _____

2. Write the ingredients from Part 1 that are probably in it. In class, tell your partner about the dish.

   _____   _____   _____

   _____   _____   _____

   _____   _____   _____

Part 3

Imagine you want to make the dish in Part 2. Which ingredients do you need to buy?

   _____   _____   _____

   _____   _____   _____

Lesson 26   **67**

27 Do you eat a big lunch?

Part 1

Unscramble each of the things people eat and drink.

1. _____ ecaerl
2. _____ aydnc
3. _____ aotpto ihspc
4. _____ eadrb
5. _____ ecir
6. _____ hteccaloo
7. _____ rtuif
8. _____ saod
9. _____ ajm

10. _____ aadls
11. _____ hknecic
12. _____ astot
13. _____ effoec
14. _____ ebaeletgvs
15. _____ uecij
16. _____ akec
17. _____ ntus
18. _____ iedc eta

Part 2

Do you eat the foods in Part 1? When do you eat them? Put them in the diagram. Add one or two more things to each one of the groups. In class, with your partner talk about your answers.

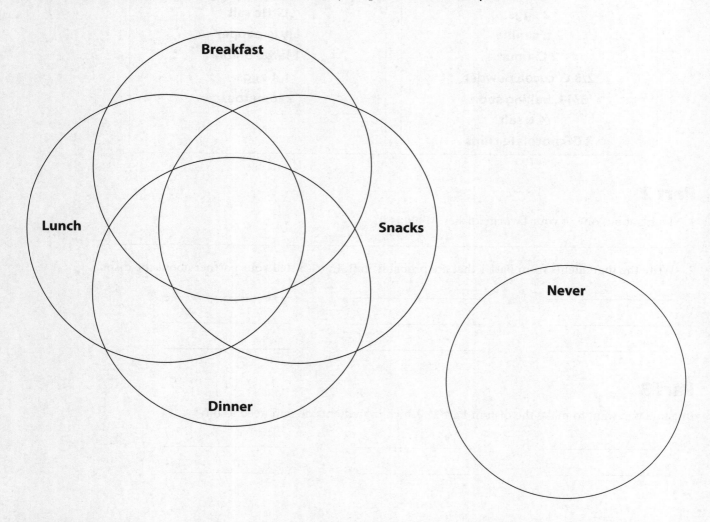

© Oxford University Press. Permission granted to reproduce for classroom use.

28 How does it taste?

Part 1

Put the words into the correct place in the puzzle.

| bitter | sweet | oily | sour | salty | bland | spicy |

Part 2

Write a clue for each word. In class, compare answers with a partner.

Across

1. _____

3. _____

4. _____

5. _____

Down

1. _____

2. _____

4. _____

Part 3

Which tastes do you like? Write them in order from like the most to like the least. In class, talk about your ideas with a partner.

_____

_____

29 I had a great weekend.

Part 1

Use the words in parentheses to write sentences with information that is true for you.

1. _____ last weekend. (study)
2. _____ all day yesterday. (stay home)
3. _____ last night. (meet friends)
4. _____ last weekend. (go shopping)
5. _____ last Saturday. (see a movie)
6. _____ the day before yesterday. (get a haircut)

In class, compare answers with a partner. Ask follow-up questions.

A: Did you study last weekend?

B: No, I didn't. I went shopping and had dinner with a friend.

A: Where did you eat?

Part 2

In each conversation, there is a mistake. Cross it out and write the correct word on the line. In class, practice the correct conversations with your partner.

1. **A:** How ~~did~~ your weekend?

   B: It was great.

   _____**was**_____

2. **A:** Did you went shopping?

   B: No, I didn't.

   _____

3. **A:** How about you?

   B: I did stay home all day on Saturday.

   _____

4. **A:** My weekend was OK.

   B: What did you doing?

   _____

5. **A:** What about you? What did you do?

   B: I was watching a movie.

   _____

6. **A:** Did you do anything special on Friday?

   B: Not really. I didn't go shopping, and I didn't watched any movies.

   _____

30 What time did you call?

Part 1

Complete the sentences with information that is true for you.

1. _____ last month.
2. _____ yesterday afternoon.
3. _____ yesterday morning.
4. _____ last week.
5. _____ last year.
6. _____ the day before yesterday.
7. _____ last night.
8. _____ this morning.

In class, compare answers with a partner.

A: What did you do last month?

B: I went to that new movie with George Clooney. It was great.

Part 2

Complete the sentences with past time expressions from Part 1. You can use the expressions more than once.
In class, compare answers with a partner.

1. I studied _____.
2. I _____ friends _____.
3. I _____ a movie _____.
4. I _____ a haircut _____.
5. I _____ shopping _____.
6. I _____ out to eat _____.
7. I _____ a walk _____.
8. I _____ a shower _____.
9. I _____ e-mail _____.
10. I _____ to bed _____.
11. I _____ up early _____.
12. I _____ dinner _____.

31 You won't believe this!

Part 1

Unscramble each of the words used to react to news.

1. _____ cyras
2. _____ waluf
3. _____ nsattafci
4. _____ beleirrt

5. _____ dbielcreni
6. _____ gxiintce
7. _____ nusoregad
8. _____ zaimgna

Part 2

Use each of the words in Part 1 once and complete the conversations. In class, practice the conversations with a partner.

1.

A: How was the test?

B: _____.

A: Why? You studied all week.

B: I know, but it was _____. It was really hard!

2.

A: How was snowboarding? Did you like it?

B: Well, it was kind of _____, but it was too
_____. I don't think I'll go again.

3.

A: How was your trip?

B: It was _____. The food was
_____, and the people were
_____. They helped me every time I got lost.
I want to go back again!

4.

A: You won't believe this! I just went bungee jumping! It was
great!

B: It sounds _____ to me. I don't think I'll try!

32 What are your plans?

Part 1

Write one or two words to complete each activity. If a word is not needed, write an X. Then match each activity to its meaning.

1. _____ for a test   A. go see people who are your family

2. _____ up late   B. go to a place outside to play

3. _____ the mall   C. watch people play games

4. _____ out of town   D. go to a place to see beautiful pictures

5. _____ watch sports   E. go to a place where you can shop

6. _____ to a park   F. go to another city

7. _____ relatives   G. not go to bed early

8. _____ a museum   H. study before a test

Part 2

How often do you do the activities in Part 1? Write the six activities you do the most often. Put them in order from most often to least often. In class, talk about your ideas with a partner.

_____

_____

Part 3

Complete the conversations with your own plans. In class, practice the conversations with a partner.

1.

Mo Lin: What are your plans for tonight?

You: _____.

2.

Massimo: What are you going to do after class?

You: _____.

3.

Collin: What are you doing tomorrow night?

You: _____.

4.

Max: Are you doing anything fun this weekend?

You: _____.

Vocabulary Worksheet Answer Keys

Vocabulary Worksheet 1

Part 1
Answers will vary. Sample answer.
My first name is George.
My last name is Smith.
My middle name is Francis. / I don't have a middle name.

Part 2
1. How are you doing, Mao?
   OK. Good night.
2. Hello.
   I'm fine, thank you.
3. Not bad.
4. Goodbye

Vocabulary Worksheet 2

Part 1
1. colleague
2. stranger
3. neighbor
4. classmate
5. boss
6. teacher
7. relative
8. friend

Part 2
Answers will vary. Sample answer.
friend   relative   colleague   boss
teacher   classmate   neighbor
stranger

Part 3
Answers will vary for second part of each conversation. Sample answer.
1. colleague
   Hi. It's a pleasure to meet you.
2. friend
   It's nice to meet you.
3. neighbor
   Hello. My name is David.

Vocabulary Worksheet 3

Part 1
Alternative answers provided in parentheses.
1. write (read, send)
2. send (write, read)
3. meet (talk)
4. ✗
5. ✗
6. ✗
7. write (read, send)
8. talk (chat)

Part 2
Answers will vary. Sample answer.
Alone: write an e-mail, write a letter
With another person: video chat, social network, meet in person, talk on the phone
Both: send a text, instant message

Vocabulary Worksheet 4

Part 1
Answers will vary. Sample answer.
1. my mom
8. my friend
3. my sister
6. my brother
2. my friends
7. my grandparents
4. my dad
5. my classmates

Part 2
All of them should be checked EXCEPT
How old are you?
What's your middle name?

Part 3
Answers will vary. Sample answer.
1. It's really beautiful today, isn't it?
   It really is.
2. Cold, huh?
   Yeah, this cloudy weather sure is terrible.

Vocabulary Worksheet 5

Part 1
Answers will vary. Sample answer.
2. I don't really like pop.
3. I don't like country at all.
4. I love hip-hop.
5. I like classical music.
6. I don't really like jazz.
7. I don't like folk at all.
8. I love techno.
9. I like heavy metal.
10. I like reggae.

Part 2
2. ~~Either~~ Neither
3. ~~neither~~ too
4. ~~Neither~~ So
5. ~~don't~~ do
6. ~~do~~ don't

Part 3
1. D   2. S   3. S
4. S   5. D   6. D

Vocabulary Worksheet 6

Part 1
Answers will vary. Sample answer.
2. actor, actress, Emma Watson
7. soccer, player, team
3. Mexican, cooking, rice balls
8. Xbox, Wii, Final Fantasy XI
4. singer, Justin Timberlake, group
5. *Harry Potter, Delirium,* author
6. cash, credit card, the mall
1. plane, tickets, trains

Part 2
Answers will vary. Sample answer.
1. My favorite movie is *We Bought a Zoo*
2. *Money Ball*
3. Justin Timberlake
4. I love Mila Kunis
5. I love *Ain't Nothing Like the Real Thing*
6. Justin Timberlake
7. Yes, I do
8. I love Final Fantasy XI

Vocabulary Worksheet 7

Part 1
Students should draw clocks showing 11:30, 3:55, 1:15, 8:45, 12:00, and 12:00.

Part 2
1. It's five after ten
2. It's ten after three
3. It's twenty after eight
4. It's twenty-five after six
5. It's twenty to eight
6. It's ten to six
7. It's twenty-five to two

Part 3
1. at half past ten (or ten thirty)
2. at one o'clock
3. at half past seven (or seven thirty)

Vocabulary Worksheet 8

Part 1
1. golf
2. bungee jumping
3. kayaking
4. wrestling
5. boring
6. boxing
7. soccer

Part 2
Answers will vary. Sample answer.
dangerous   it sounds fun

Part 3
boring   dangerous   hard

Part 4
Answers will vary. Sample answer.
With a ball: golf
Do inside with a ball: soccer
Do inside: wrestling
Do inside and very dangerous: boxing
Very dangerous: bungee jumping, rock climbing, skydiving
With a ball and very dangerous: baseball
All three:
None: kayaking, jet skiing, snowboarding, skateboarding, surfing

Vocabulary Worksheet 9

Part 1
2. grandfather
4. aunt
5. uncle

Part 2
1. grandparents
2. cousin
3. cousin
4. nephew
5. niece
6. parents

Part 3
Answers will vary. Sample answer.
1. have/don't have
2. cousin
3. brother
4. friend's daughter, 4
5. am/am not
6. sister, brother
7. have/don't have
8. have/don't have

Vocabulary Worksheet 10

Part 1
Answers will vary. Sample answer.
Positive: patient, funny, friendly
Negative: shy
Both: serious, smart, quiet, confident

Part 2
1. patient
2. friendly
3. shy
4. smart
5. confident
6. funny
7. serious

Part 3
Answers will vary. Sample answer.
1. True: 1, 3, 5, 6
2. Not true: 2, 4, 7

Vocabulary Worksheet 11

Part 1
Tops: jackets, shirts, T-shirts, sweaters, watches, bracelets, rings
Bottoms: jeans, shorts, skirts, belts
Both: dresses (bracelets, rings if students consider putting them on other parts of the body, for example, ankle bracelet)

Part 2
Answers will vary. Sample answer.
Students should add three mores kinds of clothes.
Tops: coats, turtle necks
Bottoms: pants

Part 3
1. sweaters, jackets
2. T-shirts, shorts
3. watches
4. rings
5. belts
6. dresses, skirts

Vocabulary Worksheet 12

Part 1
Students should circle:
white, red, green, blue, yellow, orange, black, brown, pink, purple, gray

Part 2
That red shirt looks good on you.

Part 3
Answers will vary. Sample answer.
1. I love to wear purple.
2. An apple is red.
3. My car is white.

Vocabulary Worksheet 13

Part 1
Answers will vary. Sample answer.
Mornings: take a shower
Afternoons: **work**
Evenings: watch TV
Mornings and Afternoons: talk on the phone
Mornings and Evenings: study
Afternoons and Evenings: exercise
All three: check e-mail, **send texts**
Never: **take a bath**

Part 2
Answers will vary. Sample answers in bold under Part 1.

Part 3
Answers will vary. Sample answer.
1. at 5:30
2. at 2:15
3. at 9:45
4. at 6:35
5. at 11:45
6. at 12:00
7. No, I don't.

Vocabulary Worksheet 14

Part 1
Alternative answers provided in parentheses.
1. go
2. ✗
3. go to
4. watch (rent)
5. go out
6. go
7. watch (play)
8. take a

Part 2
Answers will vary. Sample answer.
go out to eat   take a walk   workout
go to the library   go shopping
go to the mall   watch movies
watch sports

Part 3
Answers will vary. Sample answer.
1. go to the mall
   Who do you go with?
2. workout
   Where do you exercise?
3. go to the library
   What do you do there?
4. watch movies
   What kind of movies do you usually watch?

Vocabulary Worksheet 15

Part 1
Answers will vary. Sample answer.
Saturday-Sunday: go out with friends, stay up late, feel my worst
Monday-Friday: get up early, feel my best
Never: sleep in late, don't do much

Part 2
1. get up early
2. go out with friends
3. stay up late
4. sleep in late
5. don't do much
6. feel my best
7. feel my worst

Part 3
Answers may vary. Sample answer.
1. I get up at 1:00 p.m.
2. I go to bed at 1:00 a.m.
3. I watch TV and eat lots of snacks.
4. We usually go to the mall.
5. I take a shower first.
6. I usually go to class after lunch.
7. I usually work after dinner.
8. I usually have breakfast at 10:00.
9. After that, I usually go to class.

Vocabulary Worksheet 16

Part 1
1. math
2. psychology
3. management
4. literature
5. sociology
6. statistics
7. history
8. marketing
9. economics
10. English

Part 2
Answers will vary. Sample answer.
1. English, statistics, sociology, economics
2. English, economics, statistics
3. sociology

Part 3

economics: like to know how societies use money
statistics: like to see how two things are related
history: like to understand when and why things happened in the past
management: want to help run a company in the future
literature: like reading and writing poems
psychology: like to understand why people think the way they do
sociology: like to understand why people act certain ways

Vocabulary Worksheet 17

Part 1
1. living room
2. dining room
3. laundry room
4. bedroom
5. yard
6. bathroom
7. kitchen

Part 2
Answers will vary. Sample answer.
living room, kitchen, bathroom, bedroom

Part 3
Answers will vary. Sample answer.
living room, bedroom, kitchen, bathroom

Part 4
Answers will vary. Sample answer.
My apartment isn't big, but it isn't small.
My English classroom is very comfortable.
My place is convenient. I can walk to school.
My place isn't noisy, and it isn't too quiet.

Vocabulary Worksheet 18

Across
3. refrigerator
4. dishwasher
5. closet
6. chairs
8. bed
9. dresser
10. stove
12. sofa
Down
1. lamps
2. coffee table
7. shelves
11. TV

Vocabulary Worksheet 19

Part 1
1. D
2. J
3. E
4. B
5. A
6. C
7. H
8. F

Part 2
Answers will vary. Sample answer.
1. *Cinema South*
2. is/isn't
3. too far to walk from school
4. *C's Coffee*
5. across from the drug store
6. supermarket
7. *Well 4 You*, closest
8. on Station Street

Vocabulary Worksheet 20

1. a stadium
2. a park
3. a taxi stand
4. a bus stop
5. a subway station
6. a freeway
7. a river
8. a bridge

Vocabulary Worksheet 21

Part 1
Answers will vary. Sample answer.
2. a haircut
5. a cup of coffee
3. a movie ticket
6. bus fare
1. a taxi ride across town
4. museum admission fee

Part 2
Answers may vary. Sample answer.
1. less expensive
   Movies
2. a cup of coffee
   McCafe, coffee, $1.50, Joe's Cafe, $14
3. A taxi ride across town, $75
4. bus fare, a taxi ride across town
   A taxi ride across town, a movie ticket, a haircut

Part 3
Answers will vary. Sample answer.
a cup of coffee   movie ticket
a taxi ride across town   a haircut
museum admission fee   bus fare

Vocabulary Worksheet 22

Part 1
Answers may vary. Sample answer.
2. mascara, foundation, eye liner
3. Angry Birds, dolls, Legos
4. weights, a tread mill, golf clubs
5. computers, TVs, MP3 players
6. sofas, tables, chairs
   singles, albums, downloads
8. Wii, PS3, Xbox

Part 2
Answers will vary. Sample answer.
Not expensive: CDs
Not expensive and Buy Used: video games
Buy Used: furniture
Buy Used and Expensive: sports equipment
Expensive:
Expensive and Buy new: toys
Buy new: clothes
Buy new and Not expensive: makeup
Buy new, Expensive, and Not expensive:
Buy used, Expensive, and Not expensive:
Not expensive, Buy used, and Buy new:
Expensive, Buy used, and Buy new:
All four: electronics

Vocabulary Worksheet 23

Part 1
Answers will vary. Sample answer.
Online: magazines, flowers
In stores: energy drinks, candy
Both: vitamins
Never buy: newspapers, phone cards, gum

Part 2
1. I only shop twice a year because I want to buy when the clothes are on sale.
2. I never get flowers because I tell people not to send them to me.
3. I read business news magazines so I can understand the economy.
4. I never buy used comic books. I want to read them as soon as they come out, so I buy them new.
5. I buy gum about once a week because I chew it to stay awake.
6. No, I never use a phone card. I just call directly from my phone.
7. I read newspapers on the Internet almost every day.
8. Yes, I do. I buy candy about once a week.

Vocabulary Worksheet 24

Part 1
1. thick
2. thin
3. quiet
4. wide
5. dark
6. bright
7. noisy
8. narrow

Part 2
Answers may vary. Sample answer.
Electronics: thick, thin, fast, slow
Electronics and Places: quiet, noisy
Places: wide, narrow
Places and Furniture: dark
Furniture:
Furniture and Electronics: heavy, light
All three: cheap, expensive, small, large

Vocabulary Worksheet 25

Part 1
Answers will vary. Sample answer.
A lot: chicken, carrots, noodles, oranges
Not many/much: yogurt, nuts, beans
Never: tofu, rice, apples, bread, cheese

Part 2
2. ~~lots~~ lot
3. ~~noodle~~ noodles
4. ~~rices~~ rice
5. ~~many~~ much
6. ~~times~~ time

Part 3
Answers will vary. Sample answer.
1. S   4. S
2. S   5. S
3. S   6. D

Vocabulary Worksheet 26

Part 1
In neither: olives
In both: salt, eggs
In only one: butter, oil, tomatoes, flour,
onions, pepper

Part 2
Answers will vary. Sample answer.
Pizza: salt oil tomatoes flour
onions pepper olives

Part 3
Answers will vary. Sample answer.
tomatoes, olives

Vocabulary Worksheet 27

Part 1
1. cereal   10. salad
2. candy   11. chicken
3. potato chips   12. toast
4. bread   13. coffee
5. rice   14. vegetables
6. chocolate   15. juice
7. fruit   16. cake
8. soda   17. nuts
9. jam   18. iced tea

Part 2
Answers will vary. Sample answer.
Students' additions in bold.
Never: soda, nuts, **yogurt, apricots**
Breakfast: toast, jam, **cheese, bananas**
Breakfast and Lunch: cereal, **pasta**
Lunch: bread, **butter**
Lunch and Dinner: salad, iced tea, **water**
Dinner: vegetables, **pizza**
Dinner and Snacks: potato
chips, **crackers**
Snacks: candy, cake, **cookies**
Snacks and Breakfast: juice, **granola bars**
Breakfast, Lunch, Snacks: fruit,
gummy bears
Breakfast, Lunch, Dinner: chicken, **fish**

Lunch, Dinner, Snacks: chocolate,
hamburgers
Dinner, Snacks, Breakfast: rice, **grapes**
All four: coffee, **eggs**

Vocabulary Worksheet 28

Part 1
Across
3. bitter   4. spicy   5. bland
Down
1. sweet   2. oily   4. salty

Part 2
Answers will vary. Sample answer.
Across
1. Lemons taste like this.
3. Some chocolate and coffee are
   _____.
4. Curry, tacos, and paella can be
   _____.
5. Rice and bread are often
   _____.
Down
1. Cookies and cake are usually
   _____.
2. Foods that are fried are often
   _____.
4. Potato chips and French fries are
   often _____.

Part 3
Answers will vary. Sample answer.
spicy   sweet   sour   salty
bitter   oily   bland

Vocabulary Worksheet 29

Part 1
Answers will vary. Sample answer.
1. I studied
2. I didn't stay home
3. I didn't meet friends
4. I went shopping
5. I didn't see a movie
6. I didn't get a haircut

Part 2
2. ~~went~~ go
3. ~~did stay~~ stayed
4. ~~doing~~ do
5. ~~was watching~~ watched
6. ~~watched~~ watch

Vocabulary Worksheet 30

Part 1
Answers will vary. Sample answer.
1. I went to a festival
2. I stayed home
3. I got up late
4. I went shopping
5. I went to Florida
6. I got a haircut
7. I watched a movie
8. I ate a light breakfast

Part 2
Answers will vary. Sample answer.
1. last night
2. went shopping with, the day before
   yesterday
3. watched, this morning
4. got, last month
5. went, last week
6. didn't go, last night
7. took, yesterday afternoon
8. took, this morning
9. read, yesterday morning
10. went, late last night
11. didn't get, this morning
12. ate a delicious, the day
    before yesterday

Vocabulary Worksheet 31

Part 1
1. scary   5. incredible
2. awful   6. exciting
3. fantastic   7. dangerous
4. terrible   8. amazing

Part 2
Answers may vary, but the essence of the
conversation (positive/negative) should
be the same. Sample answer.
1. terrible, awful
2. exciting, dangerous
3. amazing, fantastic, incredible
4. scary

Vocabulary Worksheet 32

Part 1
1. prepare   H
2. stay   G
3. go to   E
4. go   F
5. ✗   C
6. go   B
7. visit   A
8. go to   D

Part 2
Answers will vary. Sample answer.
prepare for a test   stay up late
go out of town   go to the mall
watch sports   go to a park

Part 3
Answers will vary. Sample answer.
1. I'm going to go to a baseball game.
2. I'm not sure.
3. I don't have any plans.
4. No, not really.

Confidence Booster Answer Keys

- Instead of having students always be A or B, have them switch for every other Confidence Booster. This will allow them to take turns starting the conversations in Part 2.

- If some pairs finish quickly, have them personalize the material while waiting. For example, for Confidence Booster 29–32, have them take turns asking and answering questions about their personal activities for the current week.

- To challenge students, have them create one or more conversations using some or all of the responses they didn't use in Part 2. For example, for Confidence Booster 29–32, students could use the responses (underlined below) to make the following conversation.

A: You won't believe what I did this weekend. I went bungee jumping!

B: That's fantastic!

A: Yeah, bungee jumping was exciting. But then I fell while I was waiting in line for my friend to try it.

B: How awful. Are you OK?

A: Yeah, but I'm going to a museum next weekend. Waiting in line can be dangerous!

Answers

- Answers for Part 1 can be found by comparing Student A and Student B pages in the Student Book.

Pages 82 and 90
1–4   How do you spell Sarah?

2
2. b   **3.** a   **4.** a   **5.** b

Pages 83 and 91
5–8   What time is it?

2
2. b   **3.** a   **4.** a   **5.** b

Pages 84 and 92
9–12   Who is Julie's sister?

2
2. b   **3.** a   **4.** a   **5.** a

Pages 85 and 93
13–16   What time do you wake up?

2
2. b   **3.** b   **4.** a   **5.** b

Pages 86 and 94
17–20   Where is the bank?

2
2. a   **3.** b   **4.** b   **5.** a

Pages 87 and 95
21–24   How much is a bus ticket?

2
2. b   **3.** a   **4.** b   **5.** a

Pages 88 and 96
25–28   Do we have any rice?

2
2. a   **3.** b   **4.** b   **5.** a

Pages 89 and 97
29–32   What happened on Monday?

2
2. a   **3.** b   **4.** b   **5.** a